VETERANS AFFAIRS PROGRAMS

PLANNING FOR RETIREMENT

A Study Team Report
to the Task Force
on Program Review

May 31, 1985

Available in Canada through

Authorized Bookstore Agents
and other bookstores

or by mail from

Canadian Government Publishing Centre
Supply and Services Canada
Ottawa, Canada   K1A 0S9

Catalogue No. CP32-50/11-1985E   Canada: $9.25
ISBN 0-660-11981-1   Other Countries: $11.10

Price subject to change without notice

CONTENTS

FOREWORD

The Task Force on Program Review was created in September 1984 with two major objectives - better service to the public and improved management of government programs. Recognizing the desirability of involving the private sector in the work of program review, assistance from national labour, business and professional organizations was sought. The response was immediate and generous. Each of these national organizations selected one of their members to serve in an advisory capacity. These public spirited citizens served without remuneration. Thus was formed the Private Sector Advisory Committee which has been responsible for reviewing and examining all of the work of program review.

The specific program reviews have been carried out by mixed study teams composed of a balance of private sector and public sector specialists, including representatives from provincial and municipal governments. Each study team was responsible for the review of a "family" of programs and it is the reports of these study teams that are published in this series. These study team reports represent consensus, including that of the Private Sector Advisory Committee, but not necessarily unanimity among study team members, or members of the Private Sector Advisory Committee, in all respects.

The review is unique in Canadian history. Never before has there been such broad representation from outside government in such a wide-ranging examination of government programs. The release of the work of the mixed study teams is a public acknowledgement of their extraordinarily valuable contribution to this difficult task.

Study teams reviewed existing evaluations and other available analyses and consulted with many hundreds of people and organizations. The teams split into smaller groups and consulted with interested persons in the private sector. There were also discussions with program recipients, provincial and municipal governments at all levels, from officials to cabinet ministers. Twenty provincial officials including three deputy ministers were members of various study teams.

The observations and options presented in these reports were made by the study teams. Some are subjective. That was necessary and appropriate considering that the review phase of the process was designed to be completed in a little more than a year. Each study team was given three months to carry out its work and to report. The urgent need for better and more responsive government required a fresh analysis of broad scope within a reasonable time frame.

There were several distinct stages in the review process. Terms of reference were drawn up for each study team. Study team leaders and members were appointed with assistance from the Private Sector Advisory Committee and the two Task Force Advisors: Mr. Darcy McKeough and Dr. Peter Meyboom. Mr. McKeough, a business leader and former Ontario cabinet minister, provided private sector liaison while Dr. Meyboom, a senior Treasury Board official, was responsible for liaison with the public sector. The private sector members of the study teams served without remuneration save for a nominal per diem where labour representatives were involved.

After completing their work, the study teams discussed their reports with the Private Sector Advisory Committee. Subsequently, their findings were submitted to the Task Force led by the Deputy Prime Minister, the Honourable Erik Nielsen. The other members are the Honourable Michael Wilson, Minister of Finance, the Honourable John Crosbie, Minister of Justice, and the President of the Treasury Board, the Honourable Robert de Cotret.

The study team reports represent the first orderly step toward cabinet discussion. These reports outline options as seen by the respective study teams and present them in the form of recommendations to the Task Force for consideration. The reports of the study teams do not represent government policy nor are they decisions of the government. The reports provide the basis for discussion of the wide array of programs which exist throughout government. They provide government with a valuable tool in the decision-making process.

Taken together, these volumes illustrate the magnitude and character of the current array of government programs and present options either to change the nature of these programs or to improve their management. Some decisions were announced with the May budget speech, and some subsequently. As the Minister of Finance noted in the May budget speech, the time horizon for implementation of some measures is the end of the decade. Cabinet will judge the pace and extent of such change.

These study team reports are being released in the hope that they will help Canadians understand better the complexity of the issues involved and some of the optional solutions. They are also released with sincere acknowledgement to all of those who have given so generously of their time and talent to make this review possible.

TERMS OF REFERENCE
STUDY TEAM ON VETERANS AFFAIRS PROGRAMS

PURPOSE

To establish terms of reference for a mixed study team reporting to the Ministerial Task Force on Program Review concerning Veterans Affairs programs.

TERMS OF REFERENCE

The Ministerial Task Force on Program Review seeks advice and conclusions regarding a profile of the Veterans Affairs portfolio which is simpler, more understandable and more accessible to its clientele and where decision-making is decentralized as far as possible to those in direct contact with client groups. Included in this advice could be observations regarding:

The appropriateness of the present legislative and institutional framework having regard to the particular needs of veterans at this point in their life cycle.

The work of the departmental Task Force in addressing the problems identified by the "Special Committee" and suggestions regarding any activities which should be added to the responsibilities of the Task Force.

Areas of duplication of services between federal and provincial governments or between different departments and agencies of the federal government.

Groups of services that could be consolidated.

Services whose basic objective is sound but whose form should be changed.

A summary overview of the legislation that would be required to implement any of these changes.

1

The resource implications of any recommended program changes including increased costs or savings and the number and location of either increases or decreases in staff.

By means of background information to its conclusions the study team is asked to obtain answers to four sets of questions or concerns regarding beneficiaries; efficiency and overlap; gaps and omissions; and financial projections to the year 2000.

Beneficiaries

The principal beneficiaries of the Veterans Affairs portfolio and their relationship to the total veterans population.

New or expanded services which may be required to meet the needs of the veterans population.

A comparison of the services provided with those provided by the federal and/or provincial governments to an ordinary citizen with equivalent problems.

Efficiency and Overlap

Services which are particularly troublesome to beneficiaries in terms of red tape, paperwork and delays.

Illustrative cases where a beneficiary may qualify in a number of ways for Veterans Affairs services and/or other federal or provincial services and where:

the services are complementary;

the services are similar.

Cases where the services can be delivered more efficiently by private sector organizations.

Number and location of all Veterans Affairs offices.

Approaches used by other countries, in
particular the U.S. (and the conclusions of
the Grace Commission), to caring for
veterans.

Gaps and Omissions

Any omissions in cataloguing of the services
and/or benefits being provided to veterans
such as special income tax exemptions.

Financial Projections

Projections to the year 2000 for the costs of
the services and benefits provided under the
Veterans Affairs portfolio under a number of
scenarios such as different mixes of health
services, different degrees of
"harmonization" with Old Age Security and
Guaranteed Income Supplement and simpler
pension processing procedures.

LINKAGE WITH OTHER STUDIES

At the moment, besides the Task Force on the
issues identified by the Special Committee, the Department
of Veterans Affairs is preparing plans to make adjustments
to the allowances and health services to reflect the fact
that this year half the veterans will become 65 years of age
or older. As well, the Veterans Allowances are in process
of being "harmonized" with Old Age Security and Guaranteed
Income Supplement. The project team will ensure that their
work does not duplicate anything now being done by the
department and that they will use any relevant results from
the department studies.

COMPOSITION OF STUDY TEAM

The study team is being led by a senior government
official who has been appointed in consultation with the
Minister and Deputy Minister of Veterans Affairs. The Team
Director will report to both the Public Sector Adviser and
the Private Sector Liaison Adviser serving the Chairman of
the Task Force. The Director will be supported by 1-2
seconded government officials and a matching number of
private sector representatives nominated through the Private
Sector Advisory Committee. The team, or its Director, will
meet with the Public Sector and Private Sector Liaison
Advisers at their request.

WORK PROGRAM

After a review of available material on evaluations, assessments, etc., in the department, a detailed workplan will be established.

REPORTING SCHEDULE

The study team is required to report its initial findings to the Ministerial Task Force by May 31, 1985. In addition, the Task Force will receive brief progress reports on the work done at all regular meetings.

COMMUNICATIONS WITH DEPARTMENTS

Ministers of those departments directly affected by this review will be advised which programs under their jurisdiction will be looked at during the project.

LEGISLATION RELATING TO VETERANS

ACT TITLE	RESPONSIBLE ORGANIZATION(S)
Allied Veterans Benefits Act	Department of Veterans Affairs (DVA)
Children of War Dead (Education Assistance) Act	DVA
Civilian War Pensions and Allowances Act	DVA, Canadian Pension Commission (CPC), War Veterans Allowance Board (WVAB)
Department of Veterans Affairs Act	DVA
Fire Fighters War Service Benefits Act	DVA
Returned Soldiers' Insurance Act	DVA
Soldier Settlement Act	DVA
Supervisors War Service Benefits Act	DVA
Veterans Benefit Act	DVA
Veterans Insurance Act	DVA
Veterans' Land Act	DVA
Veterans Rehabilitation Act	DVA
War Service Grants Act	DVA, WVAB
War Veterans Allowance Act	DVA, WVAB
Women's Royal Naval Services and the South African Military Nursing Service (Benefits) Act	DVA
Pension Act	CPC, Pension Review Board (PRB), Bureau of Pensions Advocates (BPA)
Compensation for Former Prisoners of War Act	CPC
Special Operators War Services Benefits Act	CPC
RCMP Superannuation Act	CPC
RCMP Pension Continuation Act (Adjudication of disability and death claims)	CPC
Halifax Relief Commission Pension Continuation Act	CPC
Army Benevolent Fund Act	DVA
Reinstatement in Civil Employment Act	DVA

REGULATIONS

Assistance Fund (WVA and CWA) Regulations	DVA
Guardianship of Veterans' Property Regulations	DVA
Last Post Fund Regulations	DVA
Pensioners Training Regulations	DVA
Vetcraft Shops Regulations	DVA
Veterans Burial Regulations	DVA
Veterans Estates Regulations	DVA
Veterans Treatment Regulations	DVA
Flying Accidents Compensation Regulations	CPC
Veterans Allowance Regulations	WVAB
Civilian Allowance Regulations	WVAB
Army Benevolent Fund Regulations	DVA
Gallantry Gratuities and Annuities Order	CPC

STUDY TEAM MEMBERS

Team Leader

David Steele
Assistant Deputy Minister
Department of Supply and
    Services
Ottawa

Private Sector Members

George Neufeld
Manager
Currie, Coopers & Lybrand
Ottawa, Ont.

Ed Boston
Director
Deloitte, Haskins and Sells
Toronto

Public Sector Members

Claude LaFrance
Temporary Assignment Program
Treasury Board Secretariat
Ottawa

Elayne Van Snellenberg
Privy Council Office
Ottawa

Professional Support

Monique Mahoney
Administrative Assistant
Department of Supply and
    Services
Ottawa

—

SECTION 1
SUMMARY REPORT ON THE VETERANS AFFAIRS PORTFOLIO

INTRODUCTION

The Task Force on Program Review directed the study team on Veterans Affairs to review the Veterans Affairs portfolio according to the terms of reference previously outlined. The team commenced work on March 4, 1985, and completed its review on May 31, 1985.

This report gives the results of the team's review. The report is organized to show the present situation in the portfolio with particular emphasis on activities now in process to correct a number of identified problem areas; the study team's conclusions as to where further operating improvements might be made; and recommendations as to how these could be achieved.

Throughout the study, the team took special care not to duplicate the work now being carried out at the express direction of the Minister of Veterans Affairs, The Honourable George Hees, to correct problems in the portfolio. However, as this work is already producing significant improvements in a number of areas, it has been taken into account in the formulation of the overall recommendations.

BACKGROUND

The Veterans Affairs portfolio provides a number of services to veterans and others who are eligible for Civilian War Pensions or allowances with the objective of "providing support for the economic, social, mental and physical well-being of veterans and their dependants and other eligible persons." (For simplicity, the term 'veterans' will be used to describe all persons eligible under the Acts which form part of the Veterans Affairs portfolio.)

These services are provided by five independent legal entities, namely, the Department of Veterans Affairs, the War Veterans Allowance Board, the Canadian Pension Commission, Pension Review Board and the Bureau of Pensions Advocates. Together, they administer 27 Acts of Parliament with associated regulations as listed in Section 6. Their combined budgets for 1985/86 are $1.6 billion and 4,096 person-years.

The operation of the pensions program is presently under review as a result of the Special Committee to Study Procedures under the Pension Act (the Marin Committee) which received a number of submissions. This Committee analysed the submissions and identified 62 issues. As well, it commissioned a Touche Ross and Partners report on the pension process. Since then, the Minister of Veterans Affairs has received letters and submissions from another 150 individuals or organizations. A departmental Pension Process Task Force has identified 226 issues and corrective actions are either in process or being considered. Further details on all these studies and on a Bureau of Management Consulting report on the War Veterans Allowances are given in Section 2.

The Veterans Affairs portfolio is at an important turning point. The average age of eligible veterans is now over 65 years and their needs are those of senior citizens together with added complications due to the effects of war service.

Accordingly, the portfolio is in a state of transition as the volume of some activities is reduced and these activities are replaced by others more suited to the needs of the eligible veterans.

RESULTS OF THE REVIEW

The review of the Veterans Affairs portfolio consisted of analysing the information available within the department and agencies, collecting supplementary information in a number of areas and visiting other organizations such as the Canada Pension Plan disability benefits division, the Province of Manitoba government departments concerned with health care for senior citizens, and the U.S. Veterans Administration. From this information, conclusions have been reached as follows:

Needs of Veterans in Retirement

The average age of veterans is now over 65 years. The services and benefits provided by the Veterans Affairs portfolio should be measured against the needs of senior citizens who are also veterans. These needs would appear to be:

1. Income support and disability pensions must continue to be delivered quickly and efficiently.

While Old Age Security/Guaranteed Income Supplement provides the bulk (90%) of income support to veterans in need, good service delivery of the allowances is still required since these are still important to those in need. As well, the disability pension may become a more significant portion of a retired veteran's income, so that regular, efficient and on-time delivery becomes more important than it was while the veteran was in the labour force.

2. Veterans, like senior citizens, have an increased need for health services as they become older. 'Home' and 'Institutional' care become more important and need to be available.

3. All senior citizens become less able to travel as they become older. There is a need to provide services as close to their place of residence as possible. As the number of clients is declining, provision of local services can only be carried out economically and efficiently if such services are purchased from local institutions, provincial governments or the private sector.

The analysis in subsequent sections of the report measures current services against these needs. Where the current services do not appear to meet these needs satisfactorily, alternative methods or services are suggested. As well, opportunities to deliver the services more economically are identified.

Financial and Beneficiary Projections

Based on forecasting models in use in the portfolio and the Manitoba government experience, the financial requirements and projection of the number of beneficiaries for the next 15 years are as shown in the following table. The financial projections are in 1985/86 dollars, i.e., there has been no adjustment for inflation. Additional details are given in Section 3.

	85/86	90/91	95/96	2000/2001
Total Cost ($ Billions)	1.5	1.2	1.0	.9
Beneficiaries (Thousands)	227	203	164	140

These projections indicate that:

1. The present year represents the peak year in terms
    of expenditure, mainly due to the effect of the
    Guaranteed Income Supplement on the allowances.
    Overall expenditures will decline by 20% during
    the next five years.

2. The number of beneficiaries will decline about
    10% over the next five years and the workload will
    decline at an 8% rate (i.e. more slowly than the
    overall expenditures) due to:

    a. those persons receiving the Guaranteed Income
        Supplement will still be receiving a small
        payment from the War Veterans Allowances
        program; and

    b. after the death of a pensioner, pensions
        greater than 48% of the maximum rate are
        payable to surviving spouses who continue on
        the pension program for an average of five to
        10 years after the death of the original
        pensioner.

In summary, the financial and beneficiary projections
for the next 15 years indicate a steadily declining
expenditure in 1985/86 dollars and a slower but steady
reduction in the number of beneficiaries. It is concluded
that the portfolio's strategic plans should be aimed at
redeploying and consolidating existing resources to cope
with the changing needs of the clientele rather than
considering any increase in the resources required.

Service to Clients

The portfolio delivers four basic services to eligible
veterans, their dependants and survivors, namely, pensions,
allowances, health services and property management
services. The last three provide a satisfactory level of
service in terms of the time to process applications,
changes and inquiries. However, the pension program
services currently suffer from large backlogs. The Section
on Service Delivery gives details of all the service level
measurements. In summary, the situation in respect of the
delivery of pensions is illustrated in the table below:

Backlog in Disability Pensions Processing

	New Applications	Appeals to C.P.C.	Appeals to P.R.B.
Number	3,819	1,321	1,355
Months of Work	8	4	11

Average processing times are about equal to the number of months of work in the backlog. The Minister set up a Pension Process Task Force in the fall of 1984 and has been personally coordinating actions to reduce the backlogs. As a result, the backlog of appeals to the Canadian Pension Commission is about half the level of six months ago. However, there has been a much larger than usual number of new applications in the last six months which has somewhat nullified the efforts of the Commission to reduce the backlog in that area. The Pension Review Board is currently adding four more board members and six more staff and expects to reduce its backlog to 750 cases or four months' work by March 1986.

In addition to the reduction in backlogs and improvements already being implemented as a result of the Minister's initiatives and the work of the Pension Process Task Force, other improvements that could be considered are:

1. Changing the process for handling initial applications so that more are approved at the first level. At the present time, 30% of all initial applications are given a favourable decision. After one or more levels of appeal, a further 20% to 25% of all initial applications receive a favourable decision (i.e. 50% to 55% of all initial applications eventually receive a favourable decision).

    A sample of 100 favourable appeal decisions showed that three factors accounted for 85% of the changed decisions. These were personal appearance by the veteran, new evidence and a well-presented case by the advocate. In our view, there could have been a favourable reconsideration of the initial decision with a personal appearance by the veteran in all these cases (i.e. an appeal would not have been necessary).

2. Decentralizing the authority to hear appeals. Presently, pension appeal boards are held by sending two or three Commissioners to a district office for a period of one to five days. This means that visits to any particular office are scheduled between one and 12 months apart, depending on the number of appeals ready to be heard. The Touche Ross and Partners report identified delays in scheduling of appeals as a significant factor in the total time required for a veteran to receive a decision. These delays could be significantly reduced if a number of the commissioners were resident in the regions or district offices, depending on the workload.

3. The Department of Veterans Affairs provides support to the pension process in three key areas, namely: the Benefit Delivery System which issues the cheque, the Central Registry which controls the files, and the Outside Documentation Section which obtains military service records from the Public Archives. All three areas have had insufficient resources assigned in the past and all have had large backlogs; the first two still have some unresolved technical problems. Actions taken as a result of the Minister's initiatives and the Pension Process Task Force have reduced backlogs to a normal work-in-process level. However, the Benefit Delivery System can still normally take four to eight weeks to deliver a cheque after the Pension Commission's decision and it is using 40 more person-years than originally planned. As well, the Central Registry does not readily provide files when there is a need to interrupt the normal flow in order to answer a ministerial inquiry, to speed up a decision, or to inform the veteran of the status of his/her application.

It is our view that it is possible to decentralize the authority to hear appeals to the regional or district offices. The process can also be changed so that the veteran is asked to appear in person before the decentralized authority for those rejected first applications, where the rejection is based on insufficient evidence being presented. If this is done, then the number of appeals could be reduced and veterans will receive decisions much more quickly than they do now. There may also be some freeing of resources, but this is difficult to quantify at this time since it will be some time before the tradition of appealing diminishes.

Organizational Framework

As mentioned earlier, five independent organizations are responsible for administering the 27 Acts governing the operations of the portfolio.

Section 5 describes the areas where the organizational framework leads to either poor service or inefficiency. In summary, it shows that the present separateness of the five organizations contributes to the following problems:

1. Accountability for delivery of services is not clearly established except at the level of the Minister. The present backlogs at the Pension Commission have grown over the past few years, and it has taken the personal intervention of the Minister on a routine and regular basis to ensure that all three involved organizations work together to resolve the problems. Unless the delivery of services is made the responsibility of one organization, it is likely that the present problems will recur in the future.

2. A veteran might have to visit four different offices to receive service from the portfolio. This probably does not happen very often, but visiting two different offices probably happens quite frequently, and will do so more often as the veteran population ages. From the veteran's point of view, the portfolio is one entity designed to serve his/her needs. A 'one-stop' approach would give the veteran a better level of service.

3. While many of the district offices are co-located, they are not all in the same cities. Thus some 22 cities receive locally only one service, and 15 cities receive four services. The remaining six and four cities receive two and three services respectively.

4. Separate district offices lead to inefficiencies. The average size of district office for the department, the Canadian Pension Commission, the Bureau of Pensions Advocates and the Veterans Land Administration are 23, 8, 5 and 3 respectively.

We estimate that combining the Pension Commission and Veterans Land Administration offices with the department offices would save an estimated **44** person-years in overhead.

5.   The Pension Review Board has an 11-month backlog in handling appeals and is seeking an additional 10 person-years. At the same time, the War Veterans Allowance Board is facing a decline in the number of appeals to 300. The War Veterans Allowance Board has the capacity to hear 1,100 cases per year.

Accordingly, amalgamation of the two Boards or redeployment of the spare capacity (10 to 15 person-years) from the War Veterans Allowance Board to the Pension Review Board would make for more efficient and effective use of existing resources.

In our opinion, the existing organizational framework leads to a loss of accountability for service delivery, poor service to veterans and inefficient use of resources. This situation could be readily resolved by making one organization responsible for all aspects of service delivery for the whole portfolio. (The need to maintain the perceived independence of the Bureau of Pensions Advocates may require that that Bureau be the one exception to a one-service-delivery organization approach.)

Legislative Framework

The present legislative framework is very complex and has a number of other deficiencies such as reduced political accountability compared to other social legislation, and locked-in antiquated procedures. These are discussed in Section 6 which shows that the framework could be considerably improved by:

1.   Making the Minister responsible for all aspects of pension administration, as he is for War Veterans allowances. Presently, the War Veterans Allowance Act has a clause which makes the Minister fully responsible for all aspects of the administration, including the operation of the War Veterans Allowance Board. The Pension Act refers only vaguely to the Minister. The Canadian Pension Commission and Pension Review Board are defined as separate and independent administrative agencies.

16

2. Making the Minister able to recommend regulations on war veterans allowances to the Governor-in-Council, with or without the advice of the War Veterans Allowance Board. The Minister has no power to recommend regulations on war veterans allowances to the Governor-in-Council except on the advice of the War Veterans Allowance Board.

3. Making definitive descriptions of 'theatres of war' in either the Acts or regulations. Past decisions of the Pension Review Board and the War Veterans Allowance Board have established the present definitions. As well, an Order-in-Council provides a definition of the 'theatre of war' in Korea.

4. Making all processes part of the regulations. The Pension Act specifies many of the administrative procedures such as 'statement of case', etc. which leads to cumbersome and time-consuming administration. More modern techniques cannot be introduced without a change in legislation.

5. Combining 13 of the present Acts into one comprehensive Veterans Act. These 13 Acts all deal with some aspect of the needs of a veteran or other eligible person and can be considered in three categories, namely: those related to pensions (four Acts), those related to allowances and grants (seven Acts) and those related to rehabilitation benefits (six Acts). (Note: four Acts appear in more than one category.)

Overlap with Other Programs or Private Sector Services

As indicated in Section 7, the services to veterans overlap other federal and provincial programs in the areas of health services allowances for those over 65 years of age. In the first case, the overlap is with the federal Old Age Security/Guaranteed Income Supplement program and, in the second, it is with provincial health plans. As well, the work of the department's dental clinics and some of the routine medical examinations carried out by the Pension Commission appear to duplicate what is available in the private sector. In these areas, it is evident that:

17

1.	The "harmonization" of allowances with the Old Age Security/Guaranteed Income Supplement program will remove most of the overlap for those over 65 years of age.

	When veterans qualify for both the Guaranteed Income Supplement and the war veterans allowances, the allowances are reduced by the amount received under the Old Age Security/Guaranteed Income Supplement(OAS/GIS) program. As well, action is in progress to make the income test for the allowances as identical as possible to that for the Guaranteed Income Supplement. (Some minor anomalies will still remain.)

	The department's plans for harmonization and streamlining of the payment system are expected to lead to 140 to 170 person-years becoming available for redeployment. However, closer harmonization than that planned appears possible and this could make another 20 to 40 person-years available for redeployment.

2.	The transfer of all but one of the veterans hospitals to the provinces has eliminated the overlap in health services for all practical purposes. The department has transferred 12 hospitals to provincial jurisdiction in the period 1966 to 1983. It now operates only one hospital and two domiciliary care institutions with a total bed capacity of 1,305. It has agreements with the provinces for priority access to 4,900 beds for various categories of care. Consideration should be given to transferring the remaining institutions since, at current contract rates, the department could save $20 million per year, offset by a capital transfer cost of $50 to $100 million.

3.	The Home Care program is constructed to supplement provincial services for senior citizens to the extent necessary to provide a uniform level of service in all provinces. Presently, 5,000 veterans are participating in the Home Care program at a cost of $5 million. Provincial expenditures on the same 5,000 persons are estimated at $16 million.

4. The dental clinics operated by the department handled some 14,000 cases in 1984/85 at a cost of $3 million and 92 person-years, of which 69 are directly applicable to dental care. As well, the department paid $6 million for 28,000 dental cases handled by the veteran's dentist of choice in the private sector. The cost per case is about the same for the dental clinics and the private sector. However, 25% of the dental clinic cases are for members of the RCMP, students under the auspices of CIDA, Canada Council award holders, CUSO field staff returning from foreign assignments, etc. The department may wish to reconsider its position in respect of operating dental clinics.

5. Routine medical examinations by the Pension Commission accounted for 57% of the 18,360 examinations (or 10,460 examinations) carried out in 1984/85. About 35% of these 10,460 examinations resulted in a change in pension. Each examination costs about $230 to carry out versus $30 to $60 for a similar examination carried out under provincial medicare programs. If the veteran's own doctor were asked to complete a questionnaire at annual or bi-annual intervals and if the Commission only examined those whose condition had changed, then we estimate that about 6,600 examinations need not be carried out. This would allow about 28 person-years to be redeployed. About $1,500,000 would be saved if the provincial medicare plans paid the private sector doctors and $990,000 if the Pension Commission pays them.

Veterans' Land Act Property Management Services

The department continues to administer some 27,000 property contracts with an outstanding loan value of $200 million. The average interest rate is 7% and the average balance of loan is just over $7,000 per account. The last agreement officially terminates in the year 2007, but it is estimated that nearly all outstanding loans will have been paid off by 1995.

Since over the next three years the workload is declining at about 10% per year, the department is centralizing some of the record-keeping activities in

Charlottetown and gradually reducing the number of district and regional offices. The number of person-years dedicated to this activity will decline from 183 to 141 in that period.

In our opinion, the department could achieve the 42 person-year reduction in less than three years. As mentioned earlier, the department could consider integrating the field and district offices into the appropriate Veterans Services offices as the workload declines. As well, we believe improved efficiency in the program could make up to 30 more person-years available for reassignment.

There does not seem to be much benefit to be derived from selling the Veterans' Land Act property contracts to the private sector. The average balance of loan is very low and the low interest rate would, at today's mortgage rates, mean a discount of 40% to 50% on the outstanding loan value (i.e. the government would lose about $100 million of the outstanding balance).

Commonwealth War Graves Commission

The Commonwealth War Graves Commission marks and maintains the graves of members of the forces of the Commonwealth and the Empire who died in the two World Wars, builds memorials to the dead whose graves are unknown and keeps records and registers. Costs are shared by the six partner governments. Canada's share is 9.88% of the total cost of operation. This amounts to about $2.5 million per year which is paid by the department on behalf of the Canadian government.

The Commission operates in 140 countries commemorating 1,700,000 Commonwealth war dead. Canadian war dead number 110,000 and they are buried in 74 countries. The Commission appears to be operating in a reasonably efficient and effective mode judging by the small Canadian agency in Ottawa. There appears to be no reason to disturb the present arrangement. Further details are given in Section 9.

Comparison with U.S. Veterans Administration

The U.S. Veterans Administration is a single organizational entity with a mandate to provide disability pensions, the equivalent of an allowance to those over 65 who pass a means test, compensation to surviving dependants of a veteran who dies while on duty, or in a service-connected situation and other benefits such as loan guarantees, life insurance and education assistance.

20

Presently, seven million out of 28 million veterans receive benefits. Besides the factor of size, the significant differences from the Canadian approach are:

1. There is only one accountable organization whose administrator reports directly to the President. 'One-stop' shopping is provided for all services.

2. There is only one Board of Veterans Appeals which reports directly to the administrator.

3. The administration still operates a number of hospitals because of the lack of universal medicare in the U.S.

In summary, our review of the Veterans Affairs portfolio took place at a point of transition in the history of the portfolio as more and more of its clientele become older than 65 years of age. Actions to adjust services to the requirements of senior citizens are under way in a number of areas. As well, the move to Charlottetown has exacerbated the longstanding organizational problems of the pension program so that levels of service have deteriorated drastically. The efforts of the Minister to have the backlogs reduced and service improved are having a positive effect, as are the improvements being introduced as a result of the Pension Process Task Force set up by the Minister.

However, our review of the Veterans Affairs portfolio has indicated that:

- many of the pension service problems could be resolved if there were only one service delivery organization;
- pension applications could be processed more effectively and quickly if decision-making for appeals were decentralized and selected veterans were seen in person, if their initial applications were rejected;
- combining department, Pension Commission and Veterans' Land Act district offices could lead to a better 'one-stop' service, more complete coverage in more cities and economies of scale;
- the legislative framework could be improved to provide better political control, simpler rules and definitions and more freedom to introduce better administrative procedures;
- closer harmony with the Guaranteed Income Supplement than presently planned and more use of private sector dental and medical services could make some resources available for redeployment.

OPTIONS

The study team recommends to the Ministerial Task Force that the government consider taking the following actions:

1. **One-Service Delivery Organization**

   Make the Department of Veterans Affairs responsible for all service delivery, i.e. the Canadian Pension Commission would be responsible only for making initial and appeal decisions. This would mean transferring all resources of the Commission to the department except for the Commissioners and an appropriate secretariat.

2. **One-Stop Service**

   Combine all district offices of the department, Canadian Pension Commission and Veterans Land Administration in a 'one-stop full service' set of offices in about 32 locations.

3. **Faster Pension Decisions**

   Decentralize 10 to 15 Pension Commissioners to the regions to hear appeals and to reconsider selected first decisions by seeing the applicant and his/her advocate.

4. **One Act**

   Combine 13 of the existing 27 Acts into one Act dealing with all aspects of the Veterans Affairs portfolio. At the same time, make the Minister clearly responsible for all administration, consolidate the definition of 'theatres of war' and place all 'process' sections of present Acts in regulations.

5. **Harmonize Allowances More Closely to Guaranteed Income Supplement**

   Go further than presently planned in harmonizing the income test for war veterans allowances with that for the Guaranteed Income Supplement.

6.   Privatize Some Activities

a.   Replace 6,000 routine pension medical examinations with private sector examinations.

b.   Consider if operation of some or all of the departmental dental clinics should be phased out, and replaced by purchasing more services from private sector dentists.

7.   Transfer Remaining Health Institutions to Provinces

Negotiate with three provinces for transfer of the remaining hospital and two veterans homes.

8.   Improve Efficiency

a.   Improve the efficiency of the Veterans Land Administration.

b.   Require WVAB to reduce capacity to be more in line with present and expected appeal workload.

In summary, implementation of these recommendations should lead to better service to veterans, simpler legislation and more efficient administration. As a result, the Veterans Affairs portfolio would be able to redeploy between 100 to 215 person-years. In addition, if the remaining hospital and two veterans homes can be transferred to the provinces, the portfolio could reduce its resources by 1,350 person-years and save $20 million a year offset by a one-time capital transfer cost of $50 million to $100 million.

However, implementation needs to be very carefully planned so that there is no reduction in service to veterans and the affected staff are redeployed with a minimum of personal disruption.

CONCLUSION

This review of the Veterans Affairs portfolio has taken place while the portfolio is adjusting to the changing needs of veterans as they pass the 65 years of age threshold, and while special efforts are being made to eliminate the large backlogs which have occurred in the disability pension program. The Minister has initiated a number of actions to improve the services being given to veterans and these are beginning to have an effect.

Consequently, our review has concentrated on the next five years when the workload will start to decline and the needs of veterans will be mainly those of ordinary citizens in retirement. We believe that the portfolio can best prepare for this situation by providing a one delivery organization with one-stop decentralized service and a mandate derived mainly from one piece of legislation. We have made recommendations to this effect and have identified some potential efficiency improvements as well.

The study team wishes to thank all the many members of the staff of the Veterans Affairs portfolio who so generously gave of their time and advice. We received excellent cooperation and help from everyone we dealt with. In particular, we wish to express our thanks to The Honourable George Hees for his help in getting the study started and to all the Deputy Heads of the five agencies for their support and suggestions throughout the review.

SECTION 2
PREVIOUS STUDIES

Special Committee to Study Procedures Under
The Pension Act (Marin Committee)

OBJECTIVES*

    a.   To study all procedures relating to application for pensions and awards ... including appeals to the Pension Review Board, and in particular, to study the provisions of sections 57 and 59 to 81 inclusive of the Pension Act....

    b.   To determine whether such provisions meet the needs and requirements of veterans, members of the forces and their dependants as defined in the Pension Act....

    *Extract from Treasury Board decision TB794416 dated July 6, 1984.

AUTHORITY

Treasury Board decision number TB794416.

DESCRIPTION

The committee established a research team, commissioned a study by Touche Ross and Partners, and invited briefs and/or comments from the public. It had intended to hold public hearings in the period October to December 1984. However, in October 1984, the government decided to terminate the Committee. The briefs and submissions already received clearly indicated the problem areas and it was felt that corrective action could be completed sooner if senior management were able to concentrate its attention on this. The Committee completed and submitted a report on November 15, 1984.

The Committee received letters or submissions from some 200 individuals and seven organizations. It identified 62 issues which generally address different aspects of the following five major concerns:

The excessive delays (up to 4 years) in the pension process from initial adjudication to final appeal to the Pension Review Board should be reduced.

The pension process is administratively cumbersome and could be much improved, thereby reducing some of the delays.

A number of the Canadian Pension Commission and Pension Review Board policies are unfair to the veterans and should be changed.

A number of the medical advisers appear to exceed their role and unduly influence decisions in a negative way. It is recommended that this practice be stopped.

The Pension Act needs changing to improve the clarity and intent of certain sections.

OBSERVATIONS

Generally, the issues raised by the Marin Committee are valid and the responsible organizations in the Veterans Affairs portfolio are taking corrective action on most of them.

The Minister, The Honourable George Hees, has instituted a determined effort to reduce backlogs and, therefore, delays at every step in the process. As of May, backlogs in some areas have virtually disappeared and, in others, are being reduced.

Report by Touche Ross and Partners on Organization, Management and Administrative Processes of Pension Agencies

OBJECTIVES

To review the organization, management and administrative practices of the Canadian Pension Commission, the Bureau of Pensions Advocates and the Pension Review Board along with related elements of the Department of Veterans Affairs and Public Archives Canada.

To recommend improvements in the administration and management of these agencies.

To provide counsel to the Special Committee with respect to management matters.

AUTHORITY

The study was commissioned by the Special Committee to Study Procedures under the Pension Act (Marin Committee) approved by Treasury Board decision TB794416 dated July 6, 1984.

DESCRIPTION

The Touche Ross and Partners study took place in the period July to November 1984, with the final report being presented on November 26, 1984, to the Special Committee. The study analysed the organizational relationships between the various portfolio agencies involved in the pension process and the effect of environment, legislation and workload on the delivery of pensions. The three main points of the report were:

Action should be taken immediately to improve the capacity to handle the volume of applications in order to reduce the excessive backlogs, e.g., temporary order-in-council appointments should be made to the Pension Commission and Pension Review Board, and extra operational staff should be recruited.

Operational and processing improvements identified in the report should be implemented as soon as possible to reduce the overall process time and to increase efficiency.

27

A standard form for the first application for a
disability pension should be designed and introduced.

OBSERVATIONS

Under the direction of the Minister, the agencies of
the Veterans Affairs portfolio have taken a number of
actions to increase the capacity to deliver pensions. As a
result, backlogs have been eliminated in a number of areas
and are being progressively reduced in others.

Many of the Touche Ross and Partners' recommendations
to improve the pension delivery process have been, or are in
process of being, implemented.

The report commented on the organizational complexity
of the pension delivery process as an application moves from
one agency to another but made no recommendations as to how
this could be improved.

Review of The War Veterans Allowances Program
by The Bureau of Management Consulting

OBJECTIVES

To define, analyse and recommend administrative efficiency improvements in the War Veterans Allowance program within the existing legal framework.

To formulate recommendations for the rationalization of the administration which will require changes to the Acts and regulations.

AUTHORITY

The study was authorized by Mr. J.C. Smith, Assistant Deputy Minister, Veterans Services on July 30, 1982.

DESCRIPTION

The study was carried out in the period August 1982 to August 1983. It identified a number of areas where the efficiency of the War Veterans Allowance delivery system could be improved and the resulting resources freed up used to fund new initiatives such as the Aging Veterans Program. Specifically, the report recommended:

A change in the procedures for dealing with clients. This included more reliance on the telephone and mail and fewer home visits by counsellors to obtain information for other programs. It was estimated that 50 to 60 person-years would become available for the Aging Veterans Program.

A reduction in the number of verification points, adoption of the Guaranteed Income Supplement program accounting year for calculation of the effect of earnings on benefits, and the use of the same income test as used by the Guaranteed Income Supplement program. It was estimated that implementation of this recommendation would make another 25 to 40 person-years available for other activities.

OBSERVATIONS

Most of the recommendations given in the study were implemented during 1984, although the change in the income test and accounting year will only become effective April 1, 1986, as a change in the law was required. The number of person-years used in client counselling interviews for other programs has dropped dramatically from 65 to 25. The Aging Veterans Program is now servicing over 5,000 clients and some 100 person-years are dedicated to it.

Pension Process Task Force

OBJECTIVES

To examine issues and proposals relating to the present pension process as identified in:

individual concerns brought to the attention of the Minister;

briefs and submissions from veterans organizations and the department and pension agencies of the Veterans Affairs portfolio; and

the report on the activities of the Special Committee to Study Procedures under the Pension Act.

To identify those concerns which are amenable to immediate corrective action and/or other appropriate response, and undertake to expedite such action through the appropriate organizational channels.

To undertake, or cause to be undertaken, detailed studies on the issues and proposals, as appropriate, and to make recommendations for corrective action or change.

The recommendations accepted by the Minister will be implemented directly through and by portfolio management.

AUTHORITY

The Pension Process Task Force was established in 1984 by the Deputy Minister of Veterans Affairs at the request of the Minister. The other pension agencies provided representatives to work on the Task Force.

DESCRIPTION

The Pension Process Task Force was established in the fall of 1984 to respond to the criticisms of the Special Committee to Study Procedures under the Pension Act and to review the additional submissions and letters received by the Minister after the termination of the Committee.

The Task Force essentially completed its work in February 1985, and issued a final report on March 1, 1985. This report identifies 226 separate observations on the pension process made by the Special Committee, veterans organizations, other interested organizations and individuals. These observations have been categorized as follows:

Process

There are seven sub-categories of process covering application, adjudication, assessment, promulgation, payment, personal appearance and appeals/interpretation. There are 70 observations in this category of which 42 are in process of implementation and the balance are still being studied. Sixteen of the 70 observations require a possible change in the law.

Process Support

This category includes advocacy and pension process support. There are 39 observations of which 18 are in process of implementation and the balance are still being studied. Eight of the 39 observations may require a change in the law.

Allowances

This category has 45 observations of which 41 are in process of implementation and the balance are still under study. Three of the 45 observations may require a change in the law.

Other

This category covers items such as qualifications and selection of members of the Commission or Pension Review Board, geographical location of the agencies, effectiveness and efficiency and courtesy. There are 72 observations in this category of which 24 have either already been accomplished or are in progress and the balance are still under study. Thirty-one of the 72 observations may require a change in the law.

In summary, a little more than half the 226 observations are either already, or are in the process of being, resolved. The remainder require further study which is ongoing. As well, some 49 sections of the applicable legislation have been commented on and these comments being addressed as part of the 58 observations which require changes to the legislation.

OBSERVATIONS

The Pension Process Task Force has achieved the Minister's objective to ensure that action takes place soon as possible to resolve the problems identified by Special Committee, veterans organizations and other pe or institutions. In fact, immediate progress on more half the observations is a very creditable result.

Neither the Pension Process Task Force nor the submissions commented on the overall organization and legislative framework which, in our view, have been maj causes of the problems identified.

SECTION 3
ASSESSMENT OF PROGRAM
EXPENDITURES AND WORKLOAD

Summary and Overview

Long-Term Outlook (Year 2000)

The overall expenditures of the Veterans Programs will decrease from $1,577 million in 1985/86 to about $900 million in 2000/01. The major reasons for the decrease are:

the reduction in pensions due to the aging and hence declining size of the veteran population; and

the reduction in allowances due to the aging and hence declining size of the veteran population. Also, Old Age Security (OAS) and Guaranteed Income Supplement (GIS) bring most eligible recipients over age 65 near the allowance target income level.

These decreases are offset by relatively modest increases in expenditures for health care services due to the aging of the veteran population.

The overall requirement for person-years will decrease from 4,096 in 1985/86 to about 3,300 in 2000/01. The major reason for the decrease will be from the overall decline of the workload due to:

the aging, and hence declining size of the veteran population; and

the streamlining of the procedures for the allowance program as well as harmonization with OAS/GIS.

The transfer of the remaining three institutions to the provinces and the phasing out of the dental clinics would result in reducing the requirement for person-years to about 2,900 in 2000/01.

Shorter-Term Outlook (1990)

The present year represents the peak year in terms of expenditures mainly due to the effect of the Guaranteed Income Supplement on the allowances. Overall expenditures will decline by 20% over the next five years.

The number of beneficiaries will decline about 10% over the next 5 years (i.e. more slowly than the overall expenditures due to persons receiving the Guaranteed Income Supplement, who will still be receiving a small payment from the War Veterans Allowances program).

The current increase in workload, particularly with regard to pension applications, should be overriden by the overall decline in the number of beneficiaries. The overall workload and requirement for person-years are expected to decrease by 8% over the next five years. Transferring the remaining three institutions to the provinces would result in a further reduction of 1,352 person-years.

The following table summarizes the current and forecast expenditures for the Veterans Affairs portfolio. There is greatest uncertainty regarding the forecast of expenditures for health care since:

the department's cost for health care is dependent on those services paid for by the provinces' health care programs; and

the number of recipients is dependent on the demands of the veterans and the extent to which the availability of benefits are promoted by the department.

Following are assessments of all major Veterans Programs referred to in Table 1 together with possible options for program improvement.

Table 1
SUMMARY OF CURRENT AND FORECAST VETERANS AFFAIRS PORTFOLIO EXPENDITURES
(1985$s: expenditures in millions)

Program and activities	85/86	90/91	95/96	2000/01
Pension				
Benefits	$ 748	$ 661	$ 568	$ 470
Administration	$ 25	$ 21	$ 19	$ 17
Person-years	540	379	326	270
Allowances				
Benefits	$ 471	$ 194	$ 71	$ 37
Administration	$ 25	$ 16	$ 10	$ 8
Person-years	475	300	225	150
Health Care				
Home Care				
Benefits	$ 10	$ 24	$ 30	$ 28
Administration	$ 3	$ 5	$ 5	$ 5
Person-years	170	240	250	245
Institutional Care (1)				
Benefits	$ 143	$ 137	$ 137	$ 153
Administration	$ 47	$ 47	$ 47	$ 47
Person-years: - Service	1,352	1,352	1,352	1352
- Administration	517	517	517	517
Treatment Services (1)				
Benefits	$ 42	$ 60	$ 70	$ 80
Administration	$ 14	$ 14	$ 14	$ 14
Person-years: - Service	60	60	60	60
- Administration	189	189	189	189
Special Programs				
Benefits	$ 8	$ 8	$ 8	$ 8
Administration	$ 5	$ 4	$ 4	$ 4
Person-years	116	90	80	70
Veterans Land Administration				
Benefits	$ 2	$ 0	$ 0	$ 0
Administration	$ 7	$ 4	$ 3	$ 1
Person-years	191	125	75	30
Departmental Administration (2)				
Expenditures	$ 27	$ 27	$ 26	$ 25
Person-years	486	480	465	450
Sub Totals ($s)				
Benefits	$1,424	$1,084	$ 884	$ 776
Administration	$ 153	$ 138	$ 128	$ 121
TOTALS				
Expenditures	$1,577	$1,223	$1,012	$ 897
Person-years	4,096	3,732	3,539	3,333

Notes   1.   Person-years under Institutional Care and Treatment Services are disaggregated according to those allocated to delivering a service (e.g., hospital staff, dentists) versus those administering the provision of services (e.g., counsellors; medical advisers.) 2. Departmental Administration includes resources for the benefit pay systems for all programs. 3. Forecast Admininistration expenditures are based on forecast requirements for person-years.

Disability Pensions

OBJECTIVE

To award and pay pensions as compensation for disability and death related to military service.

AUTHORITY

The Pension Act
Civilian War Pensions and Allowances Act
Compensation for Former Prisoners of War Act
Halifax Relief Commission Pension Continuation Act
Gallantry Gratuities and Annuities Order

The Canadian Pension Commission also adjudicates upon claims for disability benefits payable under the Flying Accidents Compensation Regulations and the RCMP Pension Continuation and Superannuation Acts.

DESCRIPTION

General Information

Disability pensions are paid to eligible veterans in accordance with the degree of injury suffered by the pensioner. The pensioner can apply for an adjustment to his or her pension payment if his or her medical condition changes.

Persons who are Eligible for Pensions

Veterans are eligible for pensions if: they have disabilities arising from military service in a theatre of war or in special duty areas such as Cyprus; they have disabilities arising from service, during the Second World War, in selected groups such as air raid precaution workers and overseas welfare workers; they were prisoners of war.

Surviving spouses and dependants of a pensioner receive a pension if the pensioner died as a result of an injury or disease incurred during service and was in receipt of a pension at the rate of 48% or more at the time of death.

Amount of Pension Paid to Eligible Recipients

The maximum amount of a pension is based on a formula using the average gross salary of five categories of public servants. Pensionable disabilities are assessed on a percentage scale with a total disability being assessed at 100%. The amount of pension paid is in accordance with the assessment of the disability, the marital status and the number of dependants.

Pensions are adjusted each year in accordance with the Consumer Price Index and are not taxable. In addition, allowances may be paid to pensioners who are totally disabled and require attendance services, special appliances or clothing; the same applies to those who suffer from an exceptional incapacity. A completely disabled pensioner currently receives $13,762 per annum. The married rate is $17,202 per annum.

Proposals Affecting Pensions

Members of regular forces with disabilities are not entitled to receive a pension while still serving in the forces. It is being proposed that they should be entitled to receive a disability pension prior to retiring from the forces; the cost of such a change has not been estimated. Currently, 5% of the recipients are retired members of the regular force or survivors thereof.

BENEFICIARIES, RECIPIENTS AND EXPENDITURES

	Recipients (Thousands)	Expenditures (Millions $s)
1983/84	143	$647
1984/85	143	671
1985/86	140	687
1990/91	134	661*
1995/96	116	568*
2000/01	96	470*

* Expressed in 1985 dollars.
  These forecasts were obtained from the Canadian Pension Commission.

OBSERVATIONS

The number of recipients and level of expenditures for pensions is declining. However, their rate of decline is less than that for the number of eligible veterans due to survivors of disabled veterans who are pension recipients.

War Veterans Allowances

OBJECTIVE

To provide income support to veterans who qualify by reason of insufficient income.

AUTHORITY

War Veterans Allowance Act
Part XI of the Civilian War Pensions and Allowances Act.

DESCRIPTION

General information

Allowances are paid to eligible veterans and survivors based on an income test. The Veterans Services Branch in DVA processes all initial applications, monitors the income of recipients and revises the allowance payments where necessary. The War Veterans Allowance Board handles all appeals and provides a quality control function by reviewing selected recipient files.

Persons who are eligible for allowances

In general terms, allowances are paid to persons who are veterans of the Canadian Forces and served in a theatre of war, are receiving a disability pension for an injury or disease incurred or aggravated during wartime service, or served in selected wars, and who are 60 years of age or older (55 for females) and whose income falls below specified levels ($7,932 per annum for single persons; $12,375 for married persons).

Other persons eligible for allowances are veterans of Commonwealth and Allied Forces who meet the above criteria; civilians who served in close support of the Armed Forces; and surviving spouses and orphans of persons who received or were eligible for an allowance.

Persons may be awarded allowances at earlier ages if they meet specified "hardship" criteria.

Amount of the allowance paid to eligible recipients

The maximum amount represents a level of support that is slightly above that of a person aged over 65 and receiving both Old Age Security (OAS) and the Guaranteed Income Supplement (GIS). The rationale for this level of support is to recognize the service provided to Canada by the veteran.

Currently, the maximum allowance is:

$7,932 per annum for a single eligible veteran or surviving spouse; $12,375 per annum for a married eligible veteran. The maximum amount is slightly higher for eligible veterans who are blind or have dependants.

The amount of the allowance is based on an income test. "Other income" includes interest on investments, disability pension, annuities, retirement pensions, OAS and GIS.

Allowances are adjusted each year in accordance with the Consumer Price Index and are not taxable.

For recipients over age 65, the amount of allowance required to bring their income up to the specified levels is minimal if they are eligible for OAS and GIS. Recipients who receive OAS and GIS receive at most $1,004 per year in allowances if they are single and $600 per year if married and their spouse also receives OAS.

Proposals affecting allowances

a. Amend the Old Age Security Act to provide benefits to all widow(er)s aged 60-64.
Savings to allowance: $65-85 million per year
Status: Expected to be implemented

b. Lower the qualifying age of male veterans from 60 to that for female veterans, namely 55.
Cost: $50 million per year
Status: Discussion stage

c. Make members of the Canadian Forces, who volunteered for active duty but were assigned to

service within Canada and who served more than a
year, eligible for allowances.
Cost: $316 million per year
Status: Discussion stage

d. Enable Canadian veterans residing outside Canada
to be eligible for allowances without returning to
Canada for 12 months.
Cost: $33 million per year
Status: Discussion stage

CURRENT AND FORECAST RECIPIENTS AND EXPENDITURES

Recipients are defined as persons who are expected to
receive allowances, including both veterans and survivors.

	Recipients (Thousands)	Expenditures (Millions $s)
1983/84	84	427
1984/85	87	454
1985/86	87	452
1990/91	69	194*
1995/96	48	71*
2000/01	44	37*

* Expressed in 1985 dollars.
These forecasts were obtained from the Department of
Veterans Affairs.

OBSERVATIONS

The total annual expenditure drops off significantly by
the year 2000 due to most veterans being over age 65 and
OAS/GIS bringing most eligible recipients near the allowance
target income level. The number of allowance recipients
drops off faster than the number of pension recipients
since, while both decline due to death of the recipients and
their spouses, the number of allowance recipients also drops
off due to the income test, particularly when recipients
reach age 65.

The income test for allowances is different from that
for GIS; also, the amount of allowance is calculated on the
basis of current income whereas GIS is calculated on last
year's income. The harmonization project, currently under
way, is intended to make the administration for the
allowances and GIS similar. However, the current thrust of

this project will not eliminate all differences. Consequently, the department is now investigating alternatives, by which to fully harmonize allowances and GIS, and determining the expenditure implications.

Institutional Care

OBJECTIVE

To ensure that eligible veterans are provided with adequate institutional care, which includes Extended Adult Residential Care (Type I); Extended Nursing Care (Type II); and Chronic Care (Type III or greater).

AUTHORITY

The main legislative authority for the provision of institutional care for qualified veterans is the Department of Veterans Affairs Act.

DESCRIPTION

General Information

Since the early 1960s, all but three institutions administered by the Department of Veterans Affairs have been transferred to the provinces. The three remaining institutions are located in Montreal, Ottawa and Saskatoon. Discussions with the provinces to take over the remaining three institutions from the department is an ongoing process.

Plans are being developed to fund the construction of a new extended nursing care facility on the site of the department's institution in Montreal (i.e., Senneville). This new facility is intended to replace the existing Adult Residence at Senneville and meet the veterans' needs for nursing care in the Montreal area. The department is planning to fund the building of this facility since:

> there is a shortage of nursing homes in Montreal and in Quebec generally;

> there is a requirement for extended nursing care facilities to meet the needs of eligible veterans; and

> the existing facility at Senneville is not adequate as an adult residential (Type I) facility.

The present number, type and location of the contract beds is generally a reflection of what the department had prior to transferring the hospitals to the provinces. The facilities available no longer reflect the changing needs of the veterans. The department recognizes this problem and has recently initiated action to review the needs; compare the needs with the current contracts with the provinces; renegotiate the contracts with the provinces as necessary.

The department currently provides eligible veterans with Extended Adult Residential Care (Type I) and Extended Nursing Care (Type II) through two mechanisms:

facilities provided through departmental institutions and contracts with the provinces;

financial assistance provided through the Aging Veterans Program (AVP).

The departmental institutions and beds contracted with the provinces guarantee the availability of a known number of beds for eligible veterans. The availability of financial assistance for Extended Adult Residential and Extended Nursing Care through the Aging Veterans Program does not guarantee the availability of such care for eligible veterans if such facilities do not exist in his/her community. However, meeting the veterans' needs for institutional care through arrangements such as under AVP provides the department with more flexibility.

Veterans eligible for institutional care

a.   The department operates 3 institutions and has contracts with provincial governments for beds in provincial institutions. There are 1,305 beds in the departmental institutions and the department has 4,886 beds under contract with the provinces. Veterans have access to these beds:

for extended care if they served in a theatre of war, although the veterans who apply for a bed are generally those receiving an allowance or who would be eligible for an allowance if it were not for OAS/GIS;

46

for active treatment if they have a disability pension and require hospitalization for the pensioned condition.

b.   Veterans can also apply for financial assistance for extended stay in a Type I or II institution of their choice. The criteria for eligibility for such assistance are the same as those for home care services. This assistance is provided through the department's Aging Veterans Program.

c.   By January 1, 1988, the eligibility criteria under b. will be more restrictive than under a.

d.   Veterans receiving financial assistance to stay in a Type I or II provincial institution under the Aging Veterans Program can receive a maximum of $22,000 per year. The amount paid to the eligible veteran is determined in the same manner as for home care services, namely:

   assessing the veteran's health and social needs;

   identifying the total cost of staying in the appropriate institution (in the veteran's home community if possible);

   deducting those costs that are covered by provincial programs.

   The following provides a comparison of annual bed costs to the department.

	Types I or II	Type III
Dept. Institution	$21,400	$36,400
Contract with Prov. Gov't	24,300*	5,700
Aging Veterans Program	4,500	Not Avail. Under AVP

* Estimate of magnitude based on available information.

   The costs of the contract beds, presented in the foregoing table, do not include the payments for construction and maintenance to the provinces under the transfer agreements which amounted to $19 million, $9 million and $33 million in years 1983/84, 1984/85 and 1985/86 respectively. All obligations for these payments will have been met prior to 1990.

The cost of a departmental Type III bed is high compared to a contract Type III bed since DVA only pays those costs not covered by the provincial health care programs.

The cost of a Type I or II contract bed is high compared to a Type III contract bed. For a Type III bed, the department is generally only paying for those costs not covered by provincial health care plans. For a Type I or II bed, the department's costs are higher for two reasons:

> the provinces' health care plans do not cover as much of the costs pertaining to Type I or II care as they do for Type III care, and

> the contracts for Type I and II beds with the provinces generally require that the department pay a premium price for guaranteed access to Type I and II beds.

The cost of a Type I or II contract bed is more than under AVP since:

> AVP is a "top-up" to provincial health care programs (i.e., AVP covers that portion of the costs not covered by the province);

> the level of care for an AVP bed is generally lower and doesn't include such items as medical treatment; and

> the contracts with the provinces generally require that the department pay a premium price for guaranteed access to Type I and II beds.

CURRENT AND FORECAST RECIPIENTS AND EXPENDITURES

Recipients are defined as veterans who are expected to receive institutional care.

	Recipients (Thousands)	Actual & Forecast Expenditures (Millions $s)
1984/85	6.3	138
1985/86	6.9	143
1990/91	7.2	137*
1995/96	7.2	137*
2000/01	7.4	153*

*Expressed in 1985 dollars.

The cost per recipient/bed increases during the 1990s due to the aging of the veteran population and the increased need for chronic care. The expenditures are expected to peak around the year 2000.

The forecasts for recipients and expenditures were developed on the basis of data provided by the department. The forecasts reflect the need for Type I, II and III beds, irrespective of how they would be provided, e.g., be it through AVP, a contract bed or a bed in a departmental institution.

Provincial Government Expenditures

The following provides a rough estimate of the provinces' 1984/85 expenditures on behalf of veterans receiving institutional care benefits from the Department of Veterans Affairs:

1984/85 Provincial Expenditures ($M)

	Type I or II	Type III
Contract bed with Prov. Gov't.	Information not available*	Approx. $90M
Bed provided through AVP	Approx. $3M	Not applicable

* Expected to be significantly less than for Type III beds.

OBSERVATIONS

Ensuring that eligible veterans are provided with adequate institutional care in Type I and II facilities is provided through three mechanisms, namely:

- Aging Veterans Program
- contract beds
- departmental institutions.

The transfer of the departmental institutions to the provinces has evolved to the point where all but three of the institutions have been transferred and the obligations for construction and maintenance for institutions already transferred will have been met by 1990. Furthermore, the transfers generally resulted in the department contracting for beds in former departmental institutions.

The department is now approaching a new phase since:

the number, type and location of contract beds no longer meet the needs;

the provinces are integrating former departmental institutions into their health care delivery system.

The department is generally moving towards:

using health care services provided by the provinces and private sector; and

providing eligible veterans with financial assistance for costs not covered by provincial programs.

The Aging Veterans Program is a key example of this trend.

The provinces are experiencing a general shortage of facilities for institutional care to meet the needs of the general population, although this shortage varies among and within the provinces.

OPTIONS

The study team recommends to the Task Force that the government consider providing for all types of institutional veterans care through an integrated program such as the existing Aging Veterans Program.

Contracts for beds with the provinces should:

> only be arranged where and when it is necessary to ensure that veterans have reasonable access to facilities to meet their needs;
>
> be arranged on the basis of costs for services not covered by provincial health care programs;
>
> be arranged for time frames that match the needs.

The department should complete the transfer of its institutions as soon as a reasonable transfer agreement can be negotiated with the provinces.

Contributions to the provinces for expanding existing institutions or the construction of new institutions should be made as the last resort for meeting the veterans' needs.

Home Care

OBJECTIVE

To assist eligible elderly veterans to remain as self-sufficient as possible in their own homes and thereby avoid placement in an institution.

AUTHORITY

The main legislative authority for the provision of home care for qualified veterans is the Department of Veterans Affairs Act.

DESCRIPTION

General information

Benefits for home care services are paid through the Department of Veterans Affairs' Aging Veterans Program (AVP). AVP also provides support to eligible veterans in institutions; this is dealt with in the section on Institutional Care. The Aging Veterans Program provides eligible veterans with financial assistance for costs not covered by provincial health care programs.

Veterans eligible for home care

Since April 1, 1981, disability pensioners have been eligible for home care benefits, subject to the veteran's health and social needs. Since then, eligibility has been or will be extended to allowance recipients 75 years of age and older (extended October 1, 1984); allowance recipients 65-74 years of age (to be extended January 1, 1986); disability pensioners 65 years of age and older whose receipt of OAS prevents them from receiving an allowance (to be extended January 1, 1986); veterans 65 years of age and older with theatre of war service whose receipt of OAS prevents them from receiving an allowance (to be extended January 1, 1988).

Benefits to the veteran

The maximum amount is $4,300 per year for personal care support, housekeeping and groundskeeping. Eligible veterans can also apply for benefits to cover the cost of transportation (maximum of $600 per year) and alterations to their residence to allow them to perform activities of daily living (maximum of $2,500 per residence).

The amount paid to the eligible veteran is determined by assessing the veteran's health and social needs; identifying the total cost of the appropriate home care services; deducting those costs that are covered by provincial programs.

CURRENT AND FORECAST RECIPIENTS AND EXPENDITURES

Recipients are defined as veterans who are expected to receive home care services.

	Recipients (Thousands)	Expenditures (Millions $s)
1983/84	5	5
1984/85	5	5
1985/86	7	10
1990/91	11	24*
1995/96	14	30*
2000/01	13	28*

* Expressed in 1985 dollars
These forecasts have been developed on the basis of data provided by the department and the government of the Province of Manitoba.

The average cost per recipient is currently $1,400. This is expected to increase to $2,200 during the 1990s as recipients make greater use of the available financial assistance for home care services.

Provincial Governments' Expenditures

The department's Aging Veterans Program covers costs for home care services that are not covered by the provinces' health care programs. The provincial government's expenditures are estimated to be $16 million in 1984/85 for home care services received by veterans who also received AVP. This estimate takes into account that the average AVP recipient received $1,400 in 1984/85 and that there were about 4,800 AVP recipients for home care services. The estimate also assumes that the average total annual cost per recipient for home services was $4,700 in 1984/85.

OBSERVATIONS

Provincial programs for home care services vary significantly from province to province. Without AVP, veterans in different provinces would not be provided the same level of assistance for home care services. While the provinces have implemented home care assistance programs, the level of assistance provided for home care services under AVP is more complete than that provided by any of the existing provincial programs.

The cost of home care is significantly less than for institutional care and, furthermore, provision of home care services reduces the need for placement in an institution. For example:

   The Department of National Health and Welfare conducted a study with the Manitoba Government on home care. Of the 1,167 clients admitted to the home care program in the study, they found that 822 would have been placed in an institution or remained in hospital had home care not been available.

   The Department's Aging Veterans Program provides financial assistance to recipients receiving home care as well as those placed in Type I or II institutions (i.e. adult residences or nursing homes). The average annual cost per recipient is $1,400 for home care and $4,500 for institutional care.

There is a demand for home care services. In 1984/85, approximately 95% of the AVP recipients received financial assistance for home care.

Treatment Benefits

OBJECTIVE

To ensure that eligible veterans are provided with adequate medical and dental services as well as their requirement for prescription drugs.

AUTHORITY

The main legislative authority for the provision of treatment services and benefits is the Department of Veterans Affairs Act.

DESCRIPTION

General Information

Medical and dental services are provided to eligible veterans through:

> Sixteen Department of Veterans Affairs' dental clinics;
>
> financial assistance to fully cover those costs, of services provided by non-departmental clinics, that are not covered by provincial health programs.

Similarly, financial assistance is provided to eligible veterans to fully cover those costs of prescription drugs that are not covered by provincial health programs.

Veterans who are eligible for treatment benefits

Veterans are eligible for treatment benefits if they are receiving: an allowance or would be eligible for an allowance if it weren't for OAS/GIS; a disability pension and require treatment for the pensioned condition.

These eligibility criteria are similar to those for institutional care.

Widows and other dependants are not eligible for dental services. However, other groups serviced by departmental dental clinics are members of the RCMP, students under the auspices of CIDA, Canada Council award holders, CUSO field staff returning from foreign assignments, and others at the request of other departments. These groups reimburse DVA for dental services and represented 25% of the dental visits in 1981/82.

Level of benefits provided to eligible veterans

Eligible veterans are entitled to medical services, "basic" dental services and prescription drugs. Dental treatment does not include cosmetic dentistry such as crowns and bridges unless it is essential for the health of the veteran.

Cost of treatment benefits provided in 1983/84

The total cost was $35.4 million in 1983/84. The following provides an estimated breakdown of the cost of treatment services and benefits.

	Purchased (Millions $s)	Supplied by Department (Millions $s)
Medical Services	3.2	– *
Dental Services	6.0	2.8
Prescription Drugs	16.5	–
Transportation and Related Allowances	6.9	–
	32.6	2.8

* Cost of medical doctors in departmental institutions included under Institutional Care.

The cost of medical services is relatively low since the department is only paying for those costs not covered by provincial medical programs.

CURRENT AND FORECAST EXPENDITURES

The department's expenditures on treatment benefits have increased during the past five years as indicated by the following table:

	Expenditures (Millions $s)
1980/81	21.5
1981/82	24.6
1982/83	30.4
1983/84	35.4
1984/85	40.0
1985/86	42.0 (Estimate)

56

The department estimates that these costs will reach $80-90 million (1985$s) during the late 1990s; this should be regarded as a rough estimate of future expenditures for treatment benefits.

OBSERVATIONS

Observations regarding treatment benefits all pertain to dental services:

As the average age of the veteran population increases, it will become increasingly difficult for the veterans, who are eligible for dental treatment, to have access to one of the department's 16 dental clinics. Furthermore, the cost of transportation to departmental clinics will increase as the veterans get older. Currently, 11% of all veterans are over 75 years of age; by the year 2000, 75% will be over 75 years of age.

Veterans may experience a reluctance by some private practitioners to accept an elderly or disabled patient since provincial fee schedules do not make allowance for the additional time it can take for treatment. The department plans to overcome this problem by contracting with dentists if necessary.

The department is also working with dental faculties at universities and dental associations to make them more aware of problems regarding treatment that are unique to elderly and disabled persons.

About 25% of the cases handled by the departmental dental clinics are for other than veterans. This accounts for about 15% of the dentists' time.

The department's available data makes it difficult to compare the cost and utilization of the departmental dental clinics with that of a private sector dentist.

OPTIONS

The study team recommends to the Task Force that the government reconsider present arrangements to provide dental services through the services of departmental dental clinics.

Special Programs

OBJECTIVE

To meet the various special needs of veterans and to fund various special veteran-related activities.

AUTHORITIES

There are 14 special programs and they are identified in the next section. The main legislative authority is the Department of Veterans Affairs Act, but the Veterans Insurance Act and the Children of War Dead Act cover two of the programs.

BENEFICIARIES

The special programs provide financial assistance to qualified veterans or their survivors as well as to organizations that undertake activities that benefit veterans and to maintain selected veteran memorials.

1983/84 EXPENDITURES BY PROGRAM

	Expenditures* (thousands $s)
Veterans Insurance	289
Settlement of Veterans' Estates	-**
Vetcraft Shops	300
Education Assistance	100
Commonwealth War Graves Commission	2,535
Graves and Cemeteries in Canada	180
United Nations Memorial Cemetery, Korea	21
Funerals and Burials	2,770
Last Post Fund	1,335
Services to War-blinded Veterans	125
Assistance to Needy Canadian Veterans Overseas	44
Pensioners Training	20
Canadian Red Cross	1,186
Agencies such as the Canadian Hearing Society, Canadian Paraplegic Association, Royal Canadian Legion, the Army Benevolent Fund Association of the United Kingdom Assistance Fund for Needy Veterans	2,000
TOTAL	11,000

* Excluding the cost of administering programs by
   departmental staff.
** Service provided by departmental staff but no form of
   financial assistance to the eligible veteran's estate.

Note The department's 1983/84 Annual Report provides a
   good description of each of these programs.

FUTURE EXPENDITURES

No significant net change in the expenditure level for
special programs is expected during the next 10-15 years.
However, programs for which expenditures will increase as
the age of the veteran population increases are:

Veterans Insurance
Settlement of Veterans' Estates (Administrative
   costs only)
Funerals and Burials.

Expenditures which will decrease as the age of the
veteran population increases are:

Education Assistance
Services to War-blinded Veterans
Assistance to Needy Canadian Veterans Overseas
Pensioners Training.

Expenditures which are expected to remain at current
levels are:

Vetcraft Shops
Commonwealth War Graves Commission
Graves and Cemeteries in Canada
United Nations Memorial Cemetery, Korea
Last Post Fund
Canadian Red Cross
Grants to selected organizations.

OBSERVATIONS

The program for funerals and burials overlaps with
provisions for burial assistance under the Pension Act.

There is overlap between the Assistance Fund for Needy
Veterans and the financial assistance available under the
Aging Veterans Program as it applies to Home Care Services.

59

OPTIONS

The study team recommends to the Task Force that the government consider:

- Amalgamating into one program the burial assistance currently provided under two programs.

- Amalgamating into one program the special assistance currently provided to needy veterans under two programs.

Tax Exemptions

OBJECTIVE

The objective of the various veterans' programs is to provide benefits which at this time are tax exempt.

AUTHORITY

Veterans tax exempt benefits are authorized by 27 Acts of Parliament and several Orders-in-Council.

DESCRIPTION, BENEFICIARIES AND EXPENDITURES

Considered a right acquired in wartime service and peacetime military service, veterans benefits are tax exempt. To fully assess the cost of these benefits and their impact on recipients, it is necessary to estimate the taxes that would be paid on these benefits if they were not so exempt.

All program costs used in this analysis are those of 1984/85 and the income tax rates are those of 1984 for Ontario residents. The estimates of the foregone federal and provincial taxes were prepared with the assistance of Revenue Canada (Taxation). These costs are tabulated as follows:

Type of Recipient	No.	Average Amt. of Benefit*	Estimated Fed/Prov Taxes Foregone
Allowances, single, under age 65	26,000	$ 7,922	$15,184,000
Allowances, married, under age 65	19,000	$12,375	$15,865,000
GIS "top-up" allowance, over age 65	32,000	$240 - $670	-
Pensions (average income $22,282)	132,000	$ 2,000	$57,522,000
Allowance and Pension (single)	6,300	$ 9,922	
Allowance and Pension (married)	4,600	$14,375	
TOTALS	219,900		$93,123,000

*Including dollar value of aging veteran services, where applicable.

OBSERVATIONS

It is therefore estimated that if veterans allowances, disability pensions and other portfolio benefits were not tax exempt, approximately $93.2 million in additional federal and provincial (Ontario) taxes would be perceived. Of course, some 220,000 recipients would receive that much less in benefits.

No Change

It is considered that there is no reasonable alternative to the current tax exempt situation. Levying taxes on veterans benefits would reduce the income of these 220,000 Canadians, many of whom are at or near the poverty threshold. Moreover, and most important, the government would be taking away some benefits from individuals who are deemed to have earned the gratitude of Canadians by serving their country in a time of need.

Program Administration for the
Delivery of the Disability Pension Program

Current requirement for person-years

The following table summarizes the person-years required to administer the disability pension program in 1985/86.

Number of Person-Years
(as per 1985/86 Main Estimates)

Major Activities	Canadian Pension Commission (CPC)	Bureau of Pensions Advocates (BPA)	Pension Review Board (PRB)	Totals
Management	13	1	7	21
Processing applications and appeals	118	117	18	403
Servicing current recipients	266	–	–	116
TOTAL	397	118	25	540

The major activities are defined as follows:

Management - as defined in Part III of the Main Estimates.

Processing applications and appeals - processing an application for entitlement to a pension or for a change in assessment; processing an appeal to a previous decision regarding an application; and processing enquiries related to applications and appeals.

Servicing current recipients - processing general enquiries; conducting medical examinations (both non-discretionary and discretionary); processing applications for special pension allowances such as burial assistance; counselling recipients.

Comments regarding the person-years presented in the above table are:

The person-years shown do not include an estimated 54 PYs in the Administration Branch (DVA) for operating the benefit pay system; this includes maintaining and updating recipient files in the pay system; issuing cheques; updating pension rate tables to reflect changes in Consumer Price Index; providing computer systems support to benefit pay system.

The person-years shown correspond to the 1985/86 Main Estimates and do not include the additional person-years, requested in a recent submission to Treasury Board that seeks approval, to handle the increased number of applications during the past 4-6 months. CPC is requesting an additional 27 person-years and DVA is requesting 50.

While not shown, there are some person-years associated with:

> DVA processing applications and appeals and servicing current recipients; and

> CPC operating the pension benefit pay system.

The level of these resources is not considered to be significant, although existing information systems do not report these costs.

Future requirements for person-years to support the delivery of the pension program

The CPC's workload associated with processing applications/appeals and servicing current recipients will decrease significantly over the next 15 years since:

> the total number of eligible veterans will decrease from about 675,000 in 1985 to 284,000 in the year 2000;

> the number of recipients will decrease from 140,000 in 1985 to 96,000 in the year 2000;

> the number of recipients who are widows will increase from 43,000 in 1985 to 55,000 in the year 2000. This is significant because pensioners can submit an application if they feel a change in their medical status warrants a change in the

amount of pension received, but widows' pensions
are permanently linked to their spouses' pension
level at time of death.

The person-years required to deliver the pension
program could drop from the current 540 PYs to 270 PYs by
the year 2000.

In a recent submission to Treasury Board, the CPC
is requesting additional person-years to handle the
increased number of applications as well as to
provide pensioners with more frequent medical examinations.
However, this current requirement for additional
person-years will be offset:

> due to the above-mentioned overall decrease
> in workload;
>
> by implementing the recommended improvements to
> the pension application and decision process,
> discussed elsewhere in this report;
>
> by making more use of private physicians to
> conduct medical examinations, as discussed
> elsewhere in this report.

Program Administration for the
Delivery of the War Veterans Allowance Program

Current requirement for person-years

Number of Person-Years
(as per 1985/86 Main Estimates)

Major Activities	War Veterans Allowance Board	Veterans Services Branch (DVA)	Totals
Processing applications	-	100	100
Servicing current recipients	-	340	340
Processing appeals	15	-	15
Reviewing cases	20	-	20
TOTALS	35	440	475

The major activities are defined as follows:

Processing applications - processing an application for an allowance as well as follow-up administrative work resulting from appeal cases.

Servicing current recipients - reviewing reports from recipients regarding income changes; handling inquiries; counselling recipients; processing applications for additional benefits under the Assistance Fund.

Processing appeals - self-explanatory.

Reviewing cases - selecting a sample of recipient files and reviewing them to ascertain whether the recipient is receiving the appropriate level of allowance benefit; selecting a sample of applicant files to ascertain if the appropriate decision was made regarding the application.

The person-years shown in the above table do not include an estimated 14 PYs in the department's Administration Branch for operating the benefit pay system. This includes maintaining and updating recipient files in the pay system; issuing cheques; performing pre- and post-audits; providing systems analysis support to benefit pay system.

Future requirements for person-years to support the delivery of the allowance program

Requirements in 1989/90

The requirements for PYs in 1989/90 will depend on the outcome of the initiatives currently being implemented regarding harmonization with GIS as well as what further initiatives are implemented to reduce the cost of administering the allowance program.

The attached Appendix presents the various options for reducing the cost of administering the allowance program in the Veterans Services Branch. These options are discussed elsewhere in this report under the subject of harmonization.

However, regardless of the options implemented, the PYs required by the Veterans Services Branch can be expected to decrease from the current 400 to 280 by the year 1989/90.

The PYs required by the War Veterans Allowance Board can be expected to decrease from the current 35 PYs to 20 by the year 1989/90, based on discussion elsewhere in this report regarding the Allowance Board.

The PYs required to administer the benefit pay system cannot be expected to change significantly during the next 4-5 years unless the responsibility for issuance of allowance payments is transferred to National Health and Welfare.

In summary, the PYs required to administer the Allowance Program in 1989/90 are estimated to be as follows:

PYs in 1989/90

War Veterans Allowance Board	20
Veteran Services Branch (DVA)	280
	300

67

Requirements in 2000/01

The number of allowance recipients will decrease from 69,000 in 1990/91 to 44,000 in the year 2000/01. Furthermore, the number of recipients who are age 65 and over will increase from 68% in 1990/91 to about 98% in the 2000/01.

The implementation of options B.1 or B.2 in the Appendix would reduce the required PYs to 1-2 PYs per local office and small group at headquarters, particularly if the allowance payment were to be issued by NHW. In other words, the PYs required could reach as low as 100.

The implementation of one of options A.1-A.5 would reduce the PYs required in 2000/01, relative to the PYs in 1989/90, in accordance with the number of recipients; that is, the PYs required in 2000/01 would be about 200.

In summary, the PYs required to administer the Allowance Program by the year 2000/01 could be in the range of 100-200 PYs, depending on which of the options presented in the Appendix are implemented.

OPTIONS REGARDING THE ALLOWANCE PROGRAM

OPTION	COMMENTS REGARDING OPTION	CHANGE IN EXPENDITURES FOR ALLOWANCES	PERSON YEAR REQUIREMENTS
A.1 Partial harmonization with GIS.	Currently being implemented. Includes streamlining procedures. Harmonization adopts the following GIS features: mail-in approach; adjudication and benefit control; payment and accounting year; automatic benefit calculation; automatic renewal process. Minimal impact on allowance recipients. Implementation involves transferring information by computer tape from NHW to DVA for single veterans receiving OAS/GIS and married veterans where both husband and wife are receiving OAS/GIS. The tape would provide information on about 37,000 of the 87,000 recipients.	Negligible.	• Currently require about 440 P-Ys. • Streamlining procedures will save 100 P-Ys. • Harmonization will save 40-70 P-Ys. • Net P-Y requirement is 270-300.
A.2 Partial harmonization with GIS but with extended tape transfer.	Same as option A.1 but include the following allowance recipients on the tape transferred from NHW to DVA: surviving spouse receiving OAS/GIS and married veterans whose spouse is receiving an OAS/GIS equivalent from NHW. Option A.2 would include the more complex cases compared to option A.1. It would pick up information on an additional 12,000 recipients. This option would become more significant as the age of the veteran population increases.	Negligible.	• Save an additional 13-23 P-Ys. • Net P-Y requirement is 250-290.
A.3 More complete harmonization with GIS.	Same as options A.1 and A.2 but also adopt the GIS feature of reacting only to permanent income changes. Small short-term impact on recipients; negligible longer-term impact.	Negligible.	• Save an additional 10-20 P-Ys. • Net P-Y requirement is 230-280.
A.4 Yet more complete harmonization with GIS.	Same as options A.1-A.3 but also adopt the GIS feature of exempting disability pensions, family allowances, interest and casual earnings. Recipients' allowance payments would increase.	Increase expenditures by $25-30 million over current level.	Negligible additional P-Y savings.
A.5 Complete harmonization with GIS.	Same as options A.1-A.4 but also adopt the GIS feature of deducting only $1.00 for every 2.00 of assessable income. Recipients' allowance payments would increase.	Increase expenditures by $30-40 million over current level.	Negligible additional P-Y savings.
B.1 Flat rate allowance that is tied to WVA eligibility for veterans aged 65 or over.	Includes streamlining procedures. Could adopt selected GIS features for allowance recipients under 65 but this would not result in P-Y savings in addition to those identified in A1. P-y savings would accrue from flat rate allowance paid to recipients 65 and over. Allowances for recipients 65 and over could be paid by NHW. Some recipients would lose and others would gain.	Negligible.	• Currently require about 440 P-Ys. • Streamlining procedures will save 100 P-Ys. • Flat rate allowance would save 70-90 P-Ys. • Net P-Y requirement is 250-270.
B.2 Flat rate allowance that is tied to GIS eligibility.	Similar to option B.1 except tied to GIS rather than WVA eligibility.	Increase expenditures by about $50 million over current level.	Same as for option B.1.
B.3 Flat rate allowance tied to GIS amount.	As GIS mounts decrease, the allowance would also decrease in accordance with a fixed schedule.	Increase expenditures by about $30-40 million over current year.	Approximately the same as for option B.1.

Program Administration for the
Delivery of the Health Care Services

Current requirement for person-years

The following table summarizes the person-years required to administer the health care services in 1985/86.

Major Activity	1985/86 PYs
Administering home care	170
Administering institutional care program	517
Operating departmental institutions	1,352
Administering treatment services program	189
Operating departmental dental clinics	60
TOTAL	**2,288**

The major activities are defined as follows:

Administering home care program - processing applications; monitoring recipients; counselling; processing inquiries; issuing payments to recipients; liaising with provincial health care staff.

Administering institutional care program - similar to administering home care program.

Operating departmental institutions - this pertains to the hospital in Montreal (1,192 PYs) and the nursing care facilities in Ottawa and Saskatoon (total of 160 PYs.)

Administering treatment services program - approving applications for treatment in selected cases; reviewing requests for payments.

Operating departmental dental clinics - this pertains to the department's 16 dental clinics.

**Future requirements for person-years to support the delivery
of health care services**

The requirement for PYs could decrease from the current
2,288 PYs to 876 PYs if the three remaining institutions are
transferred to the provinces and the departmental dental
clinics are phased out. There will be an increase in the
PYs required to administer the home care program. The
overall requirement for PYs to deliver health care programs
will begin to decline after the year 2000 when the need for
medical care begins to decline.

Program Administration for the Delivery of the Special Programs, Veterans Land Admininistration, and Departmental Overhead

Current requirement for person-years

The following table summarizes the person-years in these three areas:

	1985/86 PYs
Administering special programs	116
Administering the Veterans Land Administration	191
Departmental Administration	486

Departmental Administration of Veterans Affairs includes audit, evaluation, financial services, personnel services, public affairs, systems development, maintenance and operations, material management, security, records management, library, andfacilities management.

Future requirement for person-years

The requirement for person-years to administer special programs will decline moderately due to procedural improvements. No major changes in the number of recipients is foreseen.

The requirement for person-years to administer the Veterans Land Administration will decline as the size of their client-base declines.

The person-years required for departmental administration will decline in proportion to the overall size of the Veterans portfolio. However, the decline will be slower since departmental administration is made up of a number of small, largely independent staff groups that fulfil a wide range of services for the departments.

Estimates of future PY requirements are as follows:

	90/91	**95/96**	**2000/01**
Administering special programs	90	80	70
Administering the Veterans Land Administration	130	70	25
Departmental Administration	480	465	450

SECTION 4
ASSESSMENT OF SERVICE DELIVERY

Summary and Overview

General

The operating policies, procedures and practices in the Department of Veterans Affairs and in the separate agencies providing benefits to veterans and their dependants have been examined from the standpoint of service delivery. The objective of the examination has been to review those areas known to be a cause for concern to the department and to veterans alike, with a view to identifying probable causes and possible solutions.

Disability Pensions

The Canadian Pension Commission has been the target of complaints about excessive time taken to reach decisions on veterans' applications for disability pensions. This is due to the abnormally large backlog of work at the First Application and Entitlement/Assessment Board levels.

Examination of the Commission's procedural operations in the processing of first applications and appeals has indicated a number of areas that offer possibilities for improving service. The most significant prospect is an organizational change from the present centralized structure to one that allows first applications to be reconsidered at the regional level. The advocate and applicant would have the opportunity to appear in person to obtain a revised first decision which is less likely to be appealed.

Such a change would require some of the commissioners to be located at the regional offices - a move that offers other advantages such as more effective scheduling of Entitlement Boards; closer liaison with the Bureau of Pensions Advocates; and closer integration of all department services within accessible distance to the veterans.

Benefit Delivery System

The benefit delivery system has in the past contributed to the delays in service delivery in its own right. In mid-1984 the delay between promulgation of decision and the mailing of a cheque could be eight weeks or more. Some of this delay could be attributed to the move to Charlottetown and the high intake of new, untrained employees, but much of the cause had been related to internal systems deficiencies.

75

Management has succeeded in reducing the work backlog and turnaround time to less than two weeks by hiring a significant number of short-term employees. However, having achieved this objective, more cost-effective and lasting improvements need to be pursued through improved systems and employee training.

Central Registry

The Central Registry is the single most important "service" element in the total portfolio of the department. As custodian of veterans' files, its ability to control those files and assure their ready accessibility to other department/functional jurisdictions has a direct influence on the flow of work throughout the portfolio and on overall delivery performance.

Inability to obtain veterans' files from Central Registry has frequently been cited as the cause for delay in processing applications. But the real source of the problem is the number of files in circulation at any time and for periods that may exceed 12 months while awaiting processing. The Commission, in fact, uses veterans' files as its own internal production planning and workload scheduling system.

Examination reveals an urgent need to institute policies that restrict the retention of files at work stations together with an improved file control system.

War Veterans Allowances

The program review coincided with a period when the increasing proportion of veterans reached age 65 or over and became eligible for old age security and other social security benefits which rendered them ineligible for WVA programs. Notwithstanding this trend, the department has introduced organizational and procedural changes in a continuing effort to upgrade internal operations and delivery performance. These improvements are aimed at streamlining the operation and releasing person-years to meet the needs of an expanding Aging Veterans Program serving the special needs of veterans over age 65.

The War Veterans Allowances Program provides a satisfactory level of service. Examination has shown that the turnaround time for WVA applications is about 30 days, and Assistance Fund applications are decided in less than two weeks.

Health Care Services

The health care services provided under the Aging
Veterans Program are still in the process of development and
the number of recipients is projected to increase from the
1984 year-end level of less than 3,000 to 7,200 in 2 years.
In all service areas, the actual turnaround time for
completing veterans applications is less than the target
times set, and in no case is the target time more than 30
days.

Disability Pension Benefits

OBJECTIVE

To provide compensation to those veterans and serving members of the Regular Forces who have been disabled or died as a result of military service, and to their dependants. Service delivery comprises the activities of adjudication of claims, hearing appeals against unfavourable adjudications and paying regular monthly pension cheques to those who qualify.

AUTHORITY

Disability pensions are awarded and paid under the authority of:

Pension Act
Civilian War Pension and Allowances Act
RCMP Superannuation and Pension Continuation Acts
Flying Accidents Compensation Regulations
Compensation for Former Prisoners of War Act
Halifax Relief Commission Pension Continuation Act

BENEFICIARIES

As of September 1984, the number of beneficiaries under the five Acts and the Flying Accidents Compensation Regulations were:

Source of Pension	No. of Pensioners
First World War	13,637
Second World War	114,307
Special Force (Korea)	2,482
Regular Force	8,651
PoW Compensation only	2,990
Others	625
TOTAL	142,722

Service Delivery Costs

	CPC		DVA*		BPA	
	($M)	PYs	($M)	PYs	($M)	PYs
1983-84	18,0	368	4.0	119	4.4	118
1984-85	19.0	391	4.0	116	4.6	120
1985-86	19.2	397	4.3	123	4.9	118

* Benefit Delivery System only - dollars estimated.

DESCRIPTION

The responsibility for the delivery of disability pension decisions and payments is shared by four separate and independent organizations: Canadian Pension Commission; Department of Veterans Affairs; Pension Review Board and Bureau of Pensions Advocates. However, the main responsibility resides with the Canadian Pension Commission.

The procedure for processing applications for disability pensions follows the sequence:

The veteran prepares, or has prepared, an application which is submitted to the Head Office, Canadian Pension Commission. The Bureau of Pensions Advocates is a legal-aid organization that provides a free service to veterans, and the majority of applications are prepared by the Bureau on behalf of veterans. Other organizations providing a similar service to veterans are the Royal Canadian Legion and War Amputations of Canada.

The Canadian Pension Commission prepares a medical precis, from service documents contained on the veteran's file, and an "opinion" comment by a medical adviser. These documents are added to the file and the case scheduled for adjudication. All adjudications are conducted in Charlottetown.

The application is adjudicated by a Commissioner of the Canadian Pension Commission to determine whether or not the veteran is entitled to a pension within the provisions of the Act, and the level of entitlement, measured in 1/5 increments, from "0" (no entitlement) to "1" (full entitlement). Entitlement is a measure of the extent to which the veteran's physical condition is attributed to, or aggravated by, circumstances of service, and to be granted a pension it must be established that this condition has disabled the veteran.

If the adjudicator awards an entitlement, then, at the discretion of the Medical Advisory Branch, the veteran may be examined by a CPC medical examiner who recommends an assessment - to be approved by the Commission - of the extent to which the veteran is now disabled by the acknowledged physical condition. This assessment is measured in increments of 5%, from "0" to 100%. A pension award is determined by the product of entitlement and assessment (e.g., 4/5 X 50% = 40%).

If the first decision, the entitlement adjudication, is unfavourable or unacceptable, then the veteran may request a second decision (review) or alternatively, has the right to appeal, in person, to an Entitlement Board comprising two Commissioners. If an appeal is requested, it is usually initiated by the Bureau of Pensions Advocates, or other advisory organization selected by the veteran, who prepares and presents the case in person before the Board. The applicant and other witnesses may also appear to present evidence or testimony in support of the appeal. On receiving notice of a request for an Entitlement Board hearing, the Commission will prepare a Statement of Case for the benefit of the Commissioners assigned to the Board hearing.

The veteran may also appeal the assessment of the disability to an Assessment Hearing by two Commissioners. Again, the Bureau of Pensions Advocates or other organization would assume the responsibility for preparing and presenting the appeal.

If the appeal to an Entitlement Board or Assessment Hearing is unsuccessful or unacceptable to the veteran, a further final appeal may be launched - to the Pension Review Board.

OBSERVATIONS

Timeliness and Backlog

The Special Committee to Study Procedures under the Pension Act has reported on the problem of timeliness in the processing and promulgation of decisions on

80

Applications, Entitlement Boards, Assessment Hearings, Pension Review Board appeals, and the delivery of benefits after the decision has been promulgated are considered to be excessive.

These excessive turnaround times are inextricably linked with the large backlogs of work at each stage in the processing of applications, but have their source, in part, in organizational structure and the present centralization of service in Charlottetown.

The following statistical data illustrates the backlog problem:

Application Backlog and Process Time

	March 1984		March 1985	
	Appl. Pend.	Process Time Average	Appl. Pend.	Process Time Average
Canadian Pension Commission				
First Applications	1,968		3,819	
From Application receipt to First Decision		4.1 mos.		7.8 mos.
Entitlement Board Appeals	2,943		2,389	
From Application receipt to Statement of Case		2.8 mos.		5.5 mos.
From Notice of Readiness to Decision		6.3 mos.		6.5 mos.
From Decision to Promulgation		3.9 mos.		2.4 mos.
Assessment Hearings	1,290		1,048	
From Application receipt to Notice of Readiness		4.8 mos.		8.5 mos.
From Notice of Readiness to Promulgation (as for EB)		10.2 mos.		8.9 mos.
TOTAL CPC Backlog	6,201		7,256	

DVA - Benefit Delivery System

From Promulgation to Cheque Delivery (all applications)	275	2.0 mos.	275	1.0 mos.

Bureau of Pensions Advocates

First Applications From Notice of Intent to Application Submission	3,504	5.8 mos.	4,412	6.8 mos.
Entitlement Board Appeals From Statement of Case to Notice of Readiness	881	2.7 mos.	578	2.2 mos.
Assessment Board Hearings From receipt of Medical Pro-Forma to Notice of Readiness				
TOTAL BPA Backlog	4,385		4.990	

First Applications

	1982/83 (000s)	1983/84 (000s)	1984/85 (000s)
Backlog brought forward	2.8	1.1	2.1
New applications received	4.8	6.5	8.3
Applications adjudicated	6.5	5.5	6.6
Backlog carried forward	1.1	2.1	3.8*

*Recent measures taken by the Pension Commission have reduced this backlog considerably since March 1985.

The special efforts being made by the Canadian Pension Commission and the Bureau of Pensions Advocates to reduce the process times and backlogs are just beginning to take effect. It is expected that reasonable levels will be attained by mid-summer 1985.

Backlog was also an extreme problem experienced by the benefit delivery system throughout 1984, but this was overcome by the temporary employment of some 70 PYs. The present backlog is down to two weeks from about eight weeks in early 1984.

Divided Responsibility

A major factor in the build-up of the backlog has been the divided responsiblity for service delivery between the Canadian Pension Commission, the Department of Veterans Affairs and the Bureau of Pensions Advocates. An analysis of the areas with backlogs by Touche Ross and Partners (Report for the Special Committee to Study Procedures under the Pension Act) shows the points in the system where the responsibility for processing changes from one jurisdiction to another is especially prone to backlogs and delays.

Relocation of CPC Head Office

The move of the Canadian Pension Commission to Charlottetown in the summer of 1984 caused an 85% turnover of experienced staff. The lower productivity of the new staff in the early months of the move undoubtedly contributed to the build-up of the backlog.

Centralization in Charlottetown

The centralization of the Commission's processing of first applications in Charlottetown means that veterans, and advocates (or others) representing them, cannot appear in person to make their case. This leads to appeals that might have been prevented had the veteran's case been presented in person.

At the same time, the decentralization of Section 67 and Section 68 (Assessment and Entitlement) Board hearings also gives rise to the same problem because of the difficulty of scheduling visits of commissioners, now based in Charlottetown, to 32 different locations across Canada.

Records and current hearing schedules show that while some regions are visited monthly, others are visited at intervals of 12 months or longer. In some of these latter locations, the Board is unable to complete all the applications pending with the result that some, presumably, have to wait two years or longer before they are heard.

Systems

A number of system problems have contributed to the backlog. They are:

The benefit delivery system is a new computerized system installed in the Spring of 1984. Initial problems seem to have been resolved and the backlog is now down to 2 weeks. However, human resources required are 66 person-years more than original expectations.

The "single file" concept means that there are times when a number of organizational units are seeking access to the same file simultaneously, and this waiting time contributes to the generation of the backlog.

The central registry system, as it presently exists, allows for a wanted file that is in circulation to be reserved on its return to Central Registry. However, with the present large backlog and delays in processing, a file may not be returned for a year or more.

System enhancements are being made to the central registry system, but there is no assurance that they will solve all present problems.

OPTIONS

The possible alternatives suggested by the problems cited in our observations above are dealt with more fully in the section of the report titled, Decentralization of Disability Pension Decisions. The possible solutions to all these problems of inadequate service delivery have decentralization of service as a common denominator.

The CPC district office structure could be integrated with the DVA structure of regional and district offices, thus providing a "one-stop" office for veterans and permitting counselling on the complete spectrum of available benefits.

The authority for adjudications on first applications could be delegated to integrated district offices.

Entitlement and Assessment Boards could be combined and based at the DVA regional offices. This would require the deployment of commissioners and medical advisors to these offices.

With respect to shorter term solutions, the hiring of additional staff and the ad hoc appointment of additional commissioners to deplete the backlog of first applications and appeals would be more beneficial than the expedient of short-circuiting the adjudication system.

Disability Pensions
Benefit Delivery System

OBJECTIVE

To pay the amount awarded by the Canadian Pension Commission or the Pension Review Board to a veteran, and/or his or her survivors, initially and then on an ongoing basis.

AUTHORITY

The Pension Act and the Department of Veterans Affairs Act allow the department to provide support services to the Canadian Pension Commission.

DESCRIPTION

When the Canadian Pension Commission or the Pension Review Board award a pension or a special amount, the decision is sent to the Benefit Delivery Services (the organization responsible for the Benefit Delivery System) for processing as follows:

The decision is converted to a monthly amount and any retroactive payments are calculated. All of the retroactive calculations are carried out manually.

The results of the calculations are then entered into the computer system which issues a first payment for amounts owing to date (or for one-time awards) and routine monthly payments for the regular amount until directed to do otherwise. (The actual cheque is issued by the Department of Supply and Services.)

Routine status changes such as change of address, dependant reaching age of majority, etc. are also entered into the computer system. The regular monthly cheque is adjusted accordingly.

A record is kept of the amounts paid and appropriate accounting information is supplied to the Pension Commission.

BENEFICIARIES

Some 95,000 veterans and 45,000 survivors receive pension payments through the Benefit Delivery System.

EXPENDITURES

In 1985/86, Benefit Delivery Services are estimated to use 130 person-years (including seven for overtime equivalent person-years) and approximately $4.5 million. (This includes functional direction of the financial aspects of the veterans allowance payment system located in the regional offices of the department.)

OBSERVATIONS

The present system was implemented in September 1983. It appears to have a number of deficiencies which have not yet been corrected due to the move to Charlottetown. For example, there is insufficient history on the master file to allow for automatic calculation of retroactive payments – this is done manually; data entry requires complete sets of documents so that all documents in a set must be located, matched and input together; written operating procedures are inadequate so that training of new staff is difficult.

The move to Charlottetown exacerbated the technical problems by adding new and inexperienced staff. As a result, backlogs in September 1984 rose to nearly 8,000 outstanding decisions or about six weeks of work. This has now been reduced to about 3,000 or less than two weeks of work with the addition of some 70 persons.

The cut-off date for processing is the 5th to 6th of the month in which the cheque will be delivered on the 28th day (i.e. a decision issued on the 8th day of a month will result in the first cheque being delivered on the 28th day of the following month or seven to eight weeks later). There is a provision to pay widows' first cheques within 2-3 weeks through a "casual payment" procedure which is not tied to regular processing schedules. Extension of this procedure to any first award could be relatively simple.

The original 1985/86 forecast for the Benefit Delivery Services was 54 person-years. Of the 76 additional person-years being utilized in 1985/86, 56 person-years are expected to be needed on a permanent basis and the balance for reduction of the backlog and for a systems review. Even allowing for the 24.5% increase in workload since the system was designed, it appears to require some 40 person-years more than originally planned.

OPTIONS

Given the commitment of resources already made to the present benefit delivery system, the study team recommends to the Task Force that the only sensible approach is to make it work satisfactorily by:

Providing a special payment processing procedure for all first awards such as the one being used for widows in order to reduce the throughput time to two weeks or less. The Canadian Pension Commission should identify the categories of decision where a special payment procedure would be justified.

Identifying those categories of retroactive payment where it would be economical to automate the procedure and by designing and implementing an appropriate enhancement to the system.

Developing standard operating procedures and training material.

Improving the data entry procedures.

Allocating sufficient resources to enable the improvements to be made within a year to 18 months.

Central Registry

OBJECTIVE

To operate and manage the "one file" concept for the Canadian Pension Commission, the Pension Review Board, the Veterans Services Branch of the Department of Veterans Affairs, the War Veterans Allowance Board and the Bureau of Pensions Advocates.

AUTHORITY

The Department of Veterans Affairs Act allows the department to provide central services to the other four agencies and to its own Veterans Services Branch.

DESCRIPTION

At the moment, the five users can do little or no work without the file. There are about 170,000 active files in the Central Registry and, on any day, about 20,000 of them are in the hands of one of the five users. Control over the files is exercised through an on-line computer system. Users access the service as follows:

Correspondence from veterans, the Royal Canadian Legion, Members of Parliament, etc., received by the central mailroom is coded with the file number. The Central Registry then obtains the file, attaches the correspondence and sends the file to the section responsible for preparing the reply. That section is "charged" with the file until it is returned.

Applications for a pension or allowance or appeals against a decision create a request for the file from one of the four agencies or the Veterans Services Branch. The file is sent to the requestor and the computer record shows a "charge out".

As an application or appeal moves through various processing stages automatically without the file returning to the Central Registry (there can be up to 20 steps for the pension process), the file passes through control points (there are four of these) where its present whereabouts and who it is charged to are entered into the computer.

OBSERVATIONS

A "one file" central registry concept can only work well if 1% to 2% of the files are charged out at any given time. This system has about 10% of its files charged out at any given time and, because of backlogs, some of these are charged out for many months.

The present system allows a reservation to be input to the computer to interrupt the processing flow, but this occurs only when the file is returned to the Central Registry; it is not activated as the file passes through a control point. Consequently, with the present backlogs, a section not in the process flow may wait for six to 12 months before getting the file. (A system enhancement implemented on May 23, 1985 should enable reservations to be actioned at control points.)

Files are used as "production control" tools as well as for keeping documents, i.e., many sections keep the files in groups of similar pending actions such as first applications, appeals, routine examinations, etc. This means that, although a file is known to be in a particular section, it may be almost impossible to find it; it may be in any of a number of locations and/or mixed in with many other files in no particular order.

Four control points appear to be an insufficient number to keep track of, and to locate, files. The department has been reluctant to add more resources to the Central Registry operation. However, four to seven additional person years would appear to be necessary to ensure the service is satisfactory.

The file is probably not needed for all the activities. The Canadian Pension Commission has been trying out a new procedure where only copies of the essential decision documents instead of the file are sent to the Benefit Delivery System for issuance of the cheque. (This system handles 80,000 changes per year.) If similar arrangements could be made for other Pension Commission heavy users of the file such as the Medical Advisory Services (review of 10,000 routine medical examinations per year), the Communications Section (55,000 items of correspondence per year) and the Ancillary Benefits Section (30,000 decisions per year), then many of the file availability problems would disappear.

OPTIONS

There is probably no point in moving to a new filing
system since this "one file" system was introduced to
correct the problems experienced with many separate files
most of which were incomplete. However, to make the present
Central Registry system work properly, the study team
recommends that the department conduct a full scale study
to determine:

The actions which can be carried out without access to
the file if appropriate copies of the essential
documents are made.

The number, location and duties of control points
particularly for Pension Commission heavy users such as
Medical Advisory Services, Ancillary Benefits and
Communications. Added duties could include keeping
work-in-process files until the day they are needed.

The rules as to how long a file may be kept before
sending it back to Central Registry for inclusion of
recent mail, checking against a reservation list, etc.
For example, it may be that a file should be routinely
sent back to Central Registry every two weeks until a
section has completed its actions.

The need for another method of process control besides
using the physical file. This would mean that the file
need only be drawn from Central Registry the day before
it is to be worked on and it could be returned the day
after.

War Veterans Allowance/Civilian War Allowances

OBJECTIVES

To provide allowances for persons, or their dependants, who meet service and eligibility requirements and who, because of age or incapacity, have insufficient income for maintenance as determined by a modified income test.

In addition to these allowances, WVA/CWA recipients who are in need of help to meet emergencies may be eligible for other benefits, including cash grants through the Assistance Fund Program. This program provides emergency assistance in such areas as purchasing health needs, furniture, clothing and shelter.

AUTHORITY

Allowances are awarded and paid under the authority of the War Veterans Allowance Act, and Part XI, Civilian War Pensions and Allowances Act, administered by the Veterans Services Branch of the Department of Veterans Affairs.

BENEFICIARIES

The beneficiaries of the WVA/CWA programs for the past two years, and projections for 1985-86 are:

	Beneficiaries 000's	Eligible Veteran Population 000's
1983-84	84.2	377
1984-85	88.3	336
1985-86(Estimates)	87.0	324

The 1984-85 beneficiaries comprised:

	000's
Veterans	53.0
Widows	34.7
Orphans	0.6

SERVICE DELIVERY COSTS

Expenditures and person-years for operation and administration related to the delivery of social and income support allowance services are:

	Expenditure	Person-Years		
	$ Millions	Operations	Admin.	Total
1983-84	33.2	450	398	848
1984-85	35.2	458	406	864
1985-86	23.6	295	261	556

The apparent reduction in expenditure and person-years for 1985-86 is due to an adjustment between social/income support programs and health service programs.

The distribution of the person-years in operations between the main activities is as follows:

	First Awards	Account Maint.	Case Counselg.	Counselg. Other Programs
1983-84	78	192	52	45
1984-85	75	189	50	31
1985-86	78	182	48	19

DESCRIPTION

The responsibility for the delivery of the War Veterans Allowances Program rests with the Veterans Services Branch of the Department of Veterans Affairs. Bill C-39, approved by Parliament in 1984, resulted in significant changes to the decision and appeal procedures governing the operation of the War Veterans Allowance/Civilian War Allowance programs. The Veterans Allowance District Authorities (VADA) were replaced in October 1984 with a more efficient and responsive decision making structure. Regional directors general, Veterans Services Branch, have become the first level of review for appellants who are dissatisfied with initial adjudications. An improvement to the appeal process allows the Bureau of Pensions Advocates to represent clients at hearings of the War Veterans Allowance Board.

The basic steps in the War Veterans Allowance application process, now in force, are as follows:

Application for an allowance may be made by attending a DVA District office and personally, or with the assistance of a counsellor, completing an application form. When completed, the application is forwarded to Veterans Services regional office.

The application is adjudicated at regional office by a Veterans Services Entitlement Clerk who calculates the allowance and informs the applicant of the decision.

A quality control procedure is applied to all applications to ensure consistency and accuracy of decision making.

The applicant is allowed 60 days to seek redress if dissatisfied with the decision.

If the decision is favourable, and without waiting to see if the applicant seeks redress, the Entitlement Clerk calculates the allowance and a monthly remittance is sent to the applicant. (The War Veterans Allowance Board has the right to review and may alter any decision made.)

If the applicant seeks redress, the Veterans Services Regional Director General reviews the initial adjudication and advises the applicant of his ruling. (This is a new procedure; previously the first level appeal process was conducted by WVAB.)

If still dissatisfied, the applicant, or the Bureau of Pensions Advocates on his or her behalf, may file notice of intent to appeal to the WVAB within 60 days of receiving the Regional Director General's ruling, and prepare an appeal.

Within the department, the adjudiction procedures with respect to allowances are divided and categorised as "applications" or "reconsiderations", the latter being those applications for which the applicant has sought redress, but for the major part are those situations that require updating for change of circumstances.

The adjudication and appeal processes, as described for applications, applies also to reconsiderations.

Every allowance recipient is required to report immediately to the department any change in income, marital status, number of dependants or other circumstance that is likely to impact on the allowance payment. Independently of this requirement, Veterans Services Branch conducts an annual follow-up with selected clients to determine if their current status is accurately recorded and to make corrections as appropriate.

The Acts require that quarterly adjustment to allowance ceilings be made to reflect changes in the Consumer Price Index, and allowances are adjusted accordingly.

These account maintenance procedures, including reconsiderations, constitute the largest single activity of those operational person-years engaged in the social and income support programs of Veterans Services Branch.

OBSERVATIONS

Extensive work is under way to streamline the administration of the WVA/CWA Program and to harmonize certain income test features with the Guaranteed Income Supplement Program. By April 1, 1986, it is intended that both programs will be using similar definitions of income, pay and assessment year and provisions for change of circumstances.

Adoption and implementation of such common program features will allow for income declarations filed with the Department of Health and Welfare to be used by the Department of Veterans Affairs for clients of both programs. The result will be less duplication of effort, less intrusion into a client's affairs and person-year savings which can be redeployed to meet the demands of an expanding Aging Veterans Program.

Included in the streamlining of the administration of the programs are changes to implement procedures that will:

> allow the client to mail in an application directly to regional office, thus reducing the need for personal attendance at initial screening interviews. This is similar to the approach followed by the GIS program of National Health and Welfare; and

encourage the client to deal directly with the regional office rather than district office for routine changes of circumstance.

Records of volumes and average turnaround times of WVA/CWA and Assistance Fund Grants show the following trends:

	1983/84	1984/85	1985/86 Est.
No. of Applications			
WVA/CWA Applications	15,149	14,607	15,500
WVA/CWA Reconsiderations	69,687	85,789	65,000
Assist. Fund Applications	6,879	7,354	7,300
Turnaround Times - Days Average (at year end)			
WVA/CWA Applications	32.4	30.8	-
Assist. Fund Applications	20.0	11.5	-

Health Care Services

OBJECTIVES

To provide medical, surgical and dental treatment, prosthetic appliances, domiciliary care and benefits of the Aging Veterans Program to eligible veterans and other qualified persons.

To provide counselling for veterans experiencing problems of adjustment to changing social and economic conditions, and offer a level of service to assist veterans to remain independent and self-sufficient in their own communities as long as possible. Alternatively, to provide care in institutions where such care is needed.

AUTHORITY

Health care services are provided by the Veterans Services Branch of DVA under the authority of the Department of Veterans Affairs Act and various regulations under the Act.

BENEFICIARIES

Health care services are available to veterans who are in receipt of benefits for a pensionable disability and to recipients of WVA and CWA benefits. These services are also available to other veterans whose service and financial circumstances render them eligible. Health care benefits are not available to dependants.

Recipients of health care services:

	83/84	84/85	85/86
	No. at Year End	No. at Year End	No. at Year End
Hospitals/Institutions			
DVA beds (no. of patients)	1,179*	1,160	1,170
Outside institution beds (no. of patients)	5,100**	5,100	5,700

---

* Total number of beds available   1,305
** Includes AVP patients in "hospital of choice" beds paid for by the department.

AVP Recipients	2,924		5,516		7,201

Counselling Services

Assessments made	2,317		6,684		8,700
Interviews/Visits conducted	39,937		38,000		37,500

SERVICE DELIVERY COSTS

The operating costs and person-year staffing for each principal service area, for the past two years and projected for 1985/86 are:

	83/84		84/85		85/86	
	000's	PY's	$000's	PY's	$000's	PY's
DVA Hospital/ Institutions	44,228	1,144	45,945	1,192	47,361	1,192
Health-Purchased Services	104,838	---	110,509	---	113,824	---
Dept. Nursing Homes	4,954	159	5,286	163	5,395	160
District Operations	19,444	445	19,925	435	31,237	599
Administration	8,441	250	8,650	245	13,650	337
	$181,805	1,998	190,315	2,035	211,467	2,288

DESCRIPTION

Veterans Services Branch provides counselling and treatment services related to the following health care programs.

Hospital Services and Institutional Care
    DVA hospital
    DVA veterans' homes
    Contracted hospital beds

Treatment Services
    Physician of choice
    Drugs
    Dental Care: DVA clinics
                  Dentist of choice
    Optical and prosthesis aids
    Ambulance service/travelling expense
    Nursing services
    Outside hospital services

Aging Veterans Program
     Home care and institutional care; nursing care;
     preparation of meals; housekeeping; groundskeeping, low
     level institutional care in communities, etc.

     Applications for any of these services are made through
the department's intake counsellors, and the following
sequential steps are taken until the appropriate level of
service is determined in each case.

     The veteran contacts or visits the intake counsellor at
     district office, or the counsellor visits the veteran's
     place of residence for preliminary screening and to
     discuss the veteran's health needs.

     The counsellor interviews the veteran and assesses the
     type and level of service required. The veteran's
     records are checked through the data base to establish
     eligibility status. Simple inquiries may be resolved
     on the spot; those needs involving health services are
     referred to an Assessment and Review Team comprising
     the counsellor and a district office nurse. Quality
     control review of the initial assessment and decision
     is conducted by district office senior management.

     At the discretion of the Assessment and Review Team, or
     following review by district office management, the
     case may be referred to a Health Care Team, comprising
     the counsellor, nurse, physician and other specialists
     as necessary. Quality control review of assessment and
     decision of the Health Care Team is conducted by
     regional office.

     Based on the assessment, a decision is made as to the
     level of service required from the viewpoint of all
     health disciplines, and health care resources are
     identified. The client is interviewed and counselled
     on the decision, arrangement is made for the veteran to
     receive approved services and a follow-up date is
     established by the counsellor, dependent on the risk
     factor involved. The data bank is updated.

     The counsellor follows up at the established
     interval(s) to determine current status of client and
     to monitor care.

99

OBSERVATIONS

A new health services delivery model has been implemented for the assessment of clients under the Aging Veterans Programs and Veterans Care Regulations. It is expected this system will improve the quality and timeliness of the decision-making required to initiate and monitor care.

Although all but three departmental institutions were transferred to the provinces in 1960, plans are being developed for the construction of a new nursing home on the site of the Ste-Anne's Hospital to help meet veterans' needs for nursing care in the Montreal area.

An internal study has been conducted to determine if a more cost-effective and efficient alternative could be found for delivering the Drug Program. Based on experience in Atlantic Canada, where it was found that services could be provided more effectively and efficiently by transferring administration to the private sector, steps are being taken to pursue a similar arrangement in other provinces. In the meantime, this program is undergoing review from the standpoint of systems and computerization.

In addition to these advances, the aims of the department to enhance service delivery in the health care area can also be measured in terms of service turnaround times.

The present target turnaround times and actual performance are a measure of program effectiveness.

Service	Target T.A.T. days	83/84 T.A.T. days (at Y/E)	84/85 T.A.T. days (at Y/E)
Counselling Services			
Intake	1-2		
Assessment and Review Team	5-20	21-52 → 32.9	38.9
Health Care Team	15-30		
CPC requests/reports	60	N/A	40.0
Treatment Allowances	25	9.4	13.0
Veterans Travel Expenses	15	10.8	9.0
Pharmacy Accounts	30	9.0	15.0
Physicians Accounts	30	9.3	12.0

OPTIONS

In the light of recent advances to enhance quality of service, and having regard to the acceptable turnaround times achieved in service delivery, the study team has no alternatives to offer at this time.

SECTION 5
ORGANIZATIONAL FRAMEWORK

Summary and Overview

General

The current situation, in which five organizations each serve veterans with a separate organizational structure and staff, has resulted in a lower level of service and administrative inefficiencies when the portfolio is considered as a whole.

This section analyzes these problems and proposes organizational change to eliminate, or at least reduce, these built-in inefficiencies while at the same time improving or maintaining the level of service to the client.

Regional and District Office Consolidation

The separate field structures of Veterans Services, Veterans Land Administration, the Canadian Pension Commission (CPC) and the Bureau of Pensions Advocates (BPA) mean that many cities have up to four separate offices even where these are collocated. As well, some 22 cities have only one of the four services compared to 15 that have all four. A "one-stop" centre for veterans services would provide a better service level and could reduce overhead costs due to economies of scale from larger offices. (The average size of office is 23, 3, 8 and 5 for the Veterans Services, VLA, CPC and BPA respectively.)

The Veterans Services field structure is the largest whereas VLA, CPC and BPA are smaller and perform more specialized functions in addition to counselling in their field. In light of this situation, the Veterans Services could take over the VLA function and the support of the CPC. This would provide a "one-stop" service centre and produce an estimated 44 person-years for redeployment. (The Bureau of Pensions Advocates needs to maintain a clearly perceived independence from the other services.)

Decentralization of Disability Pension Decisions

More than 50 per cent of all first applications eventually receive a favourable decision but about 20 to 25 per cent require one or more appeals to do so. With the current backlog situation, this means delays of up to 18 months can occur before a veteran with a favourable decision receives any payment.

Analysis of 100 favourable appeal decisions chosen at random shows that the presence of the advocate and the applicant were the factors that most frequently resulted in changed decisions. Accordingly, it is suggested that service delivery could be improved by allowing in-person hearings attended by the advocate for reconsideration of first decisions where the rejection was based on a lack of documentary evidence.

Currently, the average elapsed time between hearings is four months or more. Decentralizing Commissioners to the regions would allow the average wait between hearings to be reduced and provide for the ready availability of Commissioners for in-person reconsiderations of unfavourable first decisions. (Due to the tradition of appealing most first decisions, there may not be much, if any, reduction in the number of appeals for a few years.)

Pension Review Board

The pension review process is currently taking approximately 14 months although the target turnaround time is six months. Of this period, approximately 10 months is taken up by the Bureau of Pensions Advocates and the Canadian Pension Commission.

A request for an additional 10 person-years has been made to the Treasury Board in order to handle the 1,300 appeals currently in the system. If this plan is approved and if appeal levels remain constant, the backlog will be cleared and turnaround times on target by 1986/87.

Amalgamation of the two appelate bodies (PRB and WVAB) could be economic if the appeal volumes follow the natural decline in the veteran population. This option would have the advantage of providing "one-stop appeal shopping" for the approximately 11,000 veterans currently receiving both allowances and pensions as well as reducing the overhead costs of operating a comprehensive appeal system.

War Veterans Allowance Board

With the decline in the number of allowance recipients and with the new review function at the regional level of DVA, the WVAB predicts a drop in appeals to 300 a year by next year. The Board proposes to use its capacity to hear 1,100 cases per year through reviews of all first declines and second level decisions by DVA as well as problem areas in routine adjudications.

A significant contrast between WVAB and PRB was noted. PRB is struggling to find resources to reduce the backlog of appeal cases while the WVAB is applying quality control processes to utilize existing capacity. It is felt that the current plan to devote 73 per cent of capacity to review DVA decisions (of which about three per cent prove to be wrong according to a preliminary survey) is excessive.

Consideration should be given to amalgamation of the two appeal bodies (see PRB above) or the phase down of the WVAB to hearing 300 appeals and reviewing a random sample of the DVA decisions. This would allow reallocation of 10 to 15 person-years.

Regional and District Office Consolidation

OBJECTIVE

The purpose of the portfolio's regional and district organizations is to deliver benefits at the local level, as close as possible to beneficiaries, to provide services of high quality.

AUTHORITY

The regional and district offices are set up under the authority of the Minister.

DESCRIPTION

As Appendix A shows, there are four decentralized organizations in the portfolio: the Veterans Services regional and district structure (37 offices and 1,398 PYs), the Veterans Land Act district structure (40 offices and 139 PYs), the Canadian Pension Commission district structure (20 offices and 148 PYs), and the Bureau of Pensions Advocates (19 offices and 92 PYs).

BENEFICIARIES*

Beneficiaries include Canadian and some Allied veterans, ex-members of the peacetime Canadian Forces, in certain circumstances their survivors, some categories of civilians who served Canada in wartime and other groups by special arrangement. The total number of Canadian veterans of the two World Wars and of Korea is estimated at 734,000. Beneficiaries of the portfolio are living across Canada and also abroad, particularly in the U.S.

Of this total client-group, the regional and district offices of the Veterans Affairs portfolio serve:

- 88,500 recipients of allowances;

---

*It should be noted that many veterans are beneficiaries of two or more sub-programs and are therefore counted more than once in the totals.

- 3,000 recipients of benefits under the Aging Veterans Program (domestic assistance, out-patient chronic health care, etc.);
- 6,200 veterans in chronic health care hospital beds, 4,900 being in contract beds and 1,300 in the department's beds;
- 27,500 VLA beneficiaries; and
- 143,000 disability pensioners and their dependants/survivors.

EXPENDITURES

The rentals for the region and district structures total $4,160,209. The other costs can be grouped as follows:

	PYs	PY costs (000's)	O & M Costs (000's)
Veterans Services	1,398	$35,020.4	$6,315.5
Veterans' Land Act (VLA)	139	3,937.5	546.9
Canadian Pension Commission (CPC)	148	3,997.6	2,078.9
Bureau of Pensions Advocates (BPA)	92	2,782.4	74.1
TOTALS	1,777	$45,737.9	$9,015.4

OBSERVATIONS

General

The separate field structures do not provide a "one-stop" center for veterans who may qualify not only for a disability pension, but also for allowances, health services and/or aging veterans benefits. Thus, many veterans have to deal with various counsellors in different offices for different kinds of benefits (in contrast, the U.S. Veterans Administration is fully integrated in this regard).

Veterans Services

The Veterans Services field structure is the largest, having two tiers which are required because of span of control and local liaison considerations. The regional

107

offices are of good size and are managing their workloads well; they use automated data processing systems wherever appropriate. The district offices deal with individual beneficiaries (counselling is a major activity); they forward information to the regional office, receiving decisions and information from it. This system could easily take over the VLA function and the support of the CPC.

VLA

The VLA structure is being phased out. It is a small and widely dispersed organization; possibilities of savings would come from a decrease of the workload rather than from integrating the field structure. VLA benefits have already been granted; the Act no longer authorizes benefits and a gradual phase-out is planned. This diminishing program element may no longer justify a separate field organization and it would be possible to transfer VLA responsibilities and the required PYs to the DVA district offices during the phase-out.

CPC

The function of the CPC district offices is limited to medical examinations for pension applications, follow-up of pensioners and some counselling responsibilities (approximately 60% of this counselling is currently carried out by DVA for the CPC). Keeping in mind that there is a DVA district office in each city where there is a CPC office, it would be possible to transfer CPC district office responsibilities and the required PYs to DVA district offices.

This rationalization would require DVA to provide services to the CPC and permit economies of scale. Essentially, DVA would be providing a service for the CPC in its district and regional offices. Collocating the CPC medical examiners and counsellors in the DVA district offices would permit a PY re-assignment estimated at 44:24 positions of office directors and managers, and one secretary and one clerk from each office.

BPA

The lawyers of the BPA are required (by law) to maintain a "solicitor-client" relationship with applicants; they must remain independent and also appear to be independent of the Canadian Pension Commission and of the department. Nonetheless, with one exception (London), they are co-located with either DVA or CPC district offices; this presents no difficulties since veterans do not usually make very much distinction between the elements of the portfolio.

OPTIONS

The study team recommends to the Task Force that the government consider adopting one, or both, of the following measures:

Integrating the VLA district structure in the DVA district and region structure.

Integrating the CPC district offices within the Veterans Services district structure to provide a "one-stop" service centre and produce 44 PYs for re-assignment.

REGIONAL AND DISTRICT OFFICES - VETERANS AFFAIRS PORTFOLIO (1984-85)

City	Veterans Services P-Ys	VLA P-Ys	CPC P-Ys	BPA	P-Ys by City Districts/Regions	Annual Rent
St-John's Nfld	(Sub-Region) 44*	Region 21	5	3*	73	$163,584
Cornerbrook	7				7	24,655
Charlottetown	11*	1*	4	2.5*	18.5	
Halifax	Region 117 District 41*	1*	10	8*	60/117	394,949
Truro		1			1	4,442
Sidney	11*	1*			12	65,981
St-John N.B.	28	2	6*	6*	42	191,528
Moncton		1			1	4,373
Campbelton	11				11	29,222
Québec	Region 108 District 27*	1*	4	5*	37/108	111,756
Montréal	51*	District 6* Field 1*	13	12*	83	20,650
Sherbrooke	7				7	18,220
Hull		1			1	
Gatineau	7				7	17,878
Toronto	Region 215 2 districts 67*		11	5*	83/215	56,814
Ottawa	40*	1*	9	6*	56	180,965
Peterborough	14*	District 3*	1**			51,927
Willowdale		Region 31* District 3*			3/31	891,302
Brampton	12				12	61,009
Thunder Bay	7*	1*			8	23,599
Windsor	11				11	50,085
North Bay	15*	2*	1**	3*	21	2,088
Barrie		1*			1	4,658
Hamilton	26*	1*	10	3*	40	171,823
Belleville		1*			1	2,888
London	34*	1*	11	7.5	53.5	37,925
Chatham		1*			1	5,404
Welland		1*			1	2,817
Guelph		1*			1	6,971
Kingston	10		8	1.5*	19.5	57,936
Winnipeg	Region 124 District 37*	District 4*	11	4.5*	56.5/124	366,289
Brandon	8*	1*			9	19,394
Saskatoon	18	Region 25* District 4*	1**	1.5	49.5	185,198
Swift Current		1			1	2,880
Regina	20*	1*	6	3*	30	144,555
Yorkton		1			1	4,841
Calgary	29		6	3.5*	38.5	230,678
Edmonton	28*	1*	6	4*	39	165,170
Red Deer		1			1	3,260
Lethbridge		1			1	
Wainwright		1			1	3,017
Vancouver	Region 108 District 55*	District 9*	20	8*	92/108	123,816
Victoria	28*	1*	5	5*	39	149,960
Penticton	14	1*			15	48,546
Prince George	8				8	24,441
Chilliwack		1			1	4,212
Kamloops		1			1	4,254
Number of offices	37	40	20	19	116	Office Rentals: $4,135,960
P-Ys	1,398	139	148	92	1,777	In addition, 4 small VLA offices: $24,249
Salaries and Wages (000's)	35,020.4	3,937.5	3,997.6	2,782.4	45,737.9	Total accommodation cost: $4,160,209
O & M (000's)	6,315.5	546.9	2,078.9	74.1	9,015.4	

* Indicates some collocation with another portfolio office; some of these are part-time, ad hoc offices.

** Sub-offices.

110

Decentralization of Disability Pension Decisions

OBJECTIVE

To ensure that decisions regarding eligibility for a disability pension are made quickly and fairly.

DESCRIPTION

Presently, the Canadian Pension Commission decides questions of eligibility for a disability pension in the following manner:

First applications are processed in Charlottetown and a commissioner makes a decision. About 30% of all first applications receive a favourable decision. Neither the veteran nor his or her advocate appear in person at this stage.

After the decision, 55% to 60% of all first applications are appealed to an Entitlement/Assessment Board held in the nearest DVA district office and consisting of two or three commissioners. About 35% of all appeals receive a favourable decision. The veteran and his or her advocate normally appear in person at the Entitlement/Assessment Board hearing.

After the appeal decision, about 33% of the appeals (20% of all applications) are appealed to the Pension Review Board. About 17% of these or 3% of all first applications obtain a favourable decision from the PRB.

OBSERVATIONS

About 50% to 55% of all first applications eventually receive a favourable decision but 20% to 25% require one or more appeals to do so. This would mean extra delays of at least two to three months if targets for process time were met, but currently, these extra delays are as much as 18 months.

A random sample of 100 files representing 157 separate decisions by Entitlement Boards, of which 111 were reclassified as favourable, was analysed. This analysis showed that the majority of these changed decisions could be attributed to one or more, and usually several, factors

which were clearly stated or inferred in the Commissioners'
written Board decision as follows:

Factors	Incidence
Credible evidence of applicant in person	54
Presentation by advocate	38
New evidence/testimony presented	37
Preference for private sector medical opinion	12
First decision overly influenced by CPC medical opinion	19
Different interpretation	24
Others	5

It should be noted that the incidence of all factors
exceeds the number of files examined because each favourable
decision often occurred due to two or more of the factors
shown. However, one or more of the first three factors
influenced the favourable decision in 85 of the cases.

It can be concluded that had the advocate been given
the opportunity to present his or her client's case in
person at a first decision hearing, and had the client also
been present for questioning, then all of these applications
would have received a favourable decision and would not have
needed an appeal hearing.

An analysis of the appeal hearings shows that, in the
32 locations where such hearings are held, the frequency of
hearings was as follows:

No. of locations	Frequency
2	Monthly
4	One to two months
7	Two to three months
7	Three to six months
4	Six to twelve months
8	Twelve months or more
TOTAL 32	

The average is four months between hearings. An
appellant may have to wait on average up to four months from
the time his or her case is ready to proceed. However, in
the present backlog situation, there are often cases not
heard during a session and these appellants have to wait a
further four months (or more) for the next session.

OBSERVATIONS

Service delivery could be very much improved by allowing in-person hearings attended by the advocate at the first decision level for those cases which are not clear cut favourable or unfavourable.

Decentralizing commissioners to the regions would allow scheduling of in-person reconsideration of first decisions and appeals to be made with a maximum elapsed time between hearings of two months.

A study should be made to see if the "in-person" additional data could be obtained by the district office staff rather than a commissioner. This would eliminate the need to schedule an "in-person" hearing by a commissioner.

Pension Review Board (PRB)

OBJECTIVE

To ensure that eligible ex-members of the Armed Forces, certain civilians and/or their respective dependants receive the full benefits of the Pension Act and related statutes.

AUTHORITY

The Pension Review Board's mandate on matters of pension entitlement, amount of pension award and the interpretation of pension legislation comes from Sections 75 to 81 of the Pension Act and related statutes.

DESCRIPTION

The Pension Review Board, established in 1971 when major revisions were made in the Pension Act, is an independent agency of the federal government reporting to Parliament through the Minister of Veterans Affairs.

Any decision of an Entitlement Board or an Assessment Board of the Canadian Pension Commission is appealable to the PRB. The PRB has the authority to determine any questions of law or fact as to whether a person is entitled under the Act. Its decisions are final and binding. It also provides interpretations of the Pension Act.

The declining veteran population will result in a decreasing workload for the Pension Review Board. This reduction will be partially offset due to the increasing number of applications from veterans survivors and ex-regular force members.

The addition of four new Board members plus six staff in 1985/86 will allow the Board to increase its hearings and decisions well beyond the number of new appeals received in the same period. Thus, the current backlog is forecast to be halved by the end of fiscal year 1985/86. The workload trend during this decade is illustrated below.

	80/81	81/82	82/83	83/84	84/85	85/86	86/87	87/88
New appeals		1241	1251	1715	1694	1500	1500	1500
Withdrawn		37	21	27	22	–	–	–
Hearings		1937	1528	1335	1595	2132	1729	1500
Decisions		NA	1450	1250	1353	2000	1800	1500
Inventory	1956	1223	925	1278	1355	723	494	494

At the present time, the pension review process is taking approximately 14 months, although the target turnaround time is six months. This includes the time from the receipt of notice of appeal to the decision letter to the appellant. Of this period, approximately 10 months is out of the control of the Pension Review Board, since the time is principally used by the Canadian Pension Commission and Bureau of Pensions Advocates. The major time-consuming processes are records management, legal research, scheduling hearings and writing the decision.

In the presentation of, and decision-making on issues involving disability pension claims, the staff and Board members are required to examine and draw from all the circumstances of the case and all of the available evidence, the link between the disability as found by medical examination and the conditions of the veteran's military service. There is a high onus placed on establishing the facts and weighing the evidence in the situation, especially in entitlement cases. Precedents are considered in approximately 20 per cent of the cases.

BENEFICIARIES

In this decade, between 1,200 and 1,700 individuals appeal to the PRB annually. Since the establishment of the Board, approximately 14,250 appeals have been received.

EXPENDITURES

Actual expenditures for 1984/85 were in the order of $930,000 with 22 person-years (PYs). Main Estimates call for an expenditure of $1.2 million and 25 PYs in 1985/86 but this may be exceeded since Treasury Board approval of the Board's request for four additional Governor-in-Council appointments and six supporting staff.

OBSERVATIONS

Appeal levels during recent months have been double the normal rate. If this trend continues, reductions in the backlog may take longer to achieve than initially projected even with the recently approved increase in resources.

Over the last two years, favourable decisions as a percent of appeals were approximately 18 percent. However, recently this rate has doubled.

It is difficult to assess the impact that improvements in the first application and Entitlement and Assessment Board activity would have on the caseload at this appeal stage since partial entitlements may be appealed upward.

The Board plans to reduce the four-month turnaround time from receipt of notice of readiness to proceed to decision letter to appellant through additional resources. Efforts are under way to speed up the decision writing and review processes as well as to hear more cases.

OPTIONS

The study team recommends to the Task Force that the government consider the following options:

Status Quo

> The level of service performance will be improved with the planned resource level as long as business volume does not increase. Once present backlogs are reduced to acceptable levels, then the future resource levels of the Board can be determined by the volume of appeals. If subsequent business volumes follow the natural decline in the veteran population, spare capacity would emerge at this appeal level. This would entail, over time, some resource savings.

Amalgamation

> Integration with the War Veterans Allowance Board could be considered as the workload for both organizations will eventually decrease in proportion to the decline in the veteran population. The object would be to maintain a viable organization dedicated to, and identified with, the appeal process for veterans while

realizing whatever administrative economies become
feasible as the volume of business declines. We do not
foresee undue problems with Board members or staff
having to understand both allowances and pensions. An
amalgamated Board would want to review the benefits and
costs of the "review process" now in place on the
allowance side. The amalgamation option would have the
advantage of providing "one-stop appeal shopping" for
the approximately 11,000 veterans currently receiving
both allowances and pensions. The timing and
presentation of the organizational change would need to
be given careful consideration.

War Veterans Allowance Board (WVAB)

OBJECTIVE

To provide an appeal forum for veterans and their dependants who feel they are wrongly denied benefits under the War Veterans Allowance Act and Part XI of the Civilian War Pensions and Allowances Act and to give policy direction to the Department of Veterans Affairs.

AUTHORITY

The statutory framework within which the Board functions is set out in the War Veterans Allowance Act, Veterans Allowance Regulations and Part XI of the Civilian War Pensions and Allowances Act.

DESCRIPTION

The WVAB's major responsibilities are to act as a court of appeal for aggrieved applicants and recipients; to review decisions of the department to ensure that adjudication is consistent with the intent of the legislation and that the legislation is applied uniformly throughout Canada and to advise the Minister on regulations under the WVA Act. The Board also provides interpretations of the legislation which serve to continuously refine the jurisprudence respecting allowances and to provide guidance to the department on adjudications.

The Board members are served by an organization headed by an Executive Director. The primary functions of the organization are to analyze cases (initiated either by a veteran's appeal or by an officer's review of previous decisions), regulations and matters for interpretation and to bring forward all relevant information for consideration by Board members. These tasks are supported by research, administrative and support services.

Recent changes in legislation have established a new departmental review process wherein dissatisfied clients would first request a formal review by the Regional Director at Veterans Services (DVA) prior to entering any appeal to the WVAB. This will have the effect of significantly reducing the appeal workload to be handled by the WVAB.

Plans are for the Board to revitalize its review activity. It will examine every case where an applicant is denied an allowance and every case where the Regional Director conducts a review. As well, it will examine a number of routine adjudications. It is the view of the Board that this will achieve the maximum justice for all applicants.

Under this plan, there will be a continued requirement for the current level of resources despite the decline in appeals, the projected declines in the number of allowance recipients and total value of allowance payments and the expectation of closer harmonization with the OAS/GIS benefits model.

The majority of cases requiring analysis by the staff and decisions by the Board members concern matters of interpretation where the Act is not clear (e.g. definition of theatre of war) or matters concerning the way the law was applied (e.g. the method of applying the income test or whether an overpayment exists).

The Board determined that an average turnaround time of 60 days per appeal was a reasonable target. In 1984/85, the average turnaround time was 82 days. The target may be reviewed in light of the establishment of the regional review level in the department. There is no backlog in the system. WVAB believes this is in large part attributable to the precedent decisions and control functions exercised by the Board.

Appeals to the WVAB are expected to be in the order of 400 per annum in 1985/86 and 300 appeals in subsequent years until 1990/91. The Board has the capacity to hear approximately 1,100 cases per year. The difference between capacity and appeals will be utilized for reviews of first level declines by DVA and first level appeals at the regional level. Any remaining capacity to hear cases will be filled from reviews of cancellations and reductions which issue from regular adjudications by Veterans Services, DVA.

BENEFICIARIES

From July 1976 to March 1985, approximately 4,047 appeals were received by the WVAB. Total cases (including appeals, reviews, referrals, etc.,) heard by the Board in this period was 11,643.

EXPENDITURES

Forecast expenditures for 1984/85 are $1.6 million and 35 authorized person-years.

OBSERVATIONS

Amalgamation of the two veterans appeal boards (WVAB and PRB) would not appear to present great difficulties. The functions of each organization are similar in terms of case analysis, research, administration and support services. The WVAB has a review function which is not shared by the PRB. The scope and complexity of the cases would not appear to require unduly specialized knowledge or skills in their preparation or hearing.

An amalgamation would have the effect of maintaining administrative efficiency as workload inevitably declines by achieving "economies of scale" in the adjudicative components and the support groups which give effect to their decisions. It would serve to retain the appeal process while, at the same time, generating appropriate reductions in the size of the organizations.

Amalgamation of the two veterans appeal Boards has been suggested by the WVAB.

A significant contrast between the WVAB and the PRB was noted. PRB is struggling to find resources to reduce the backlog of appeal cases, while the WVAB is applying quality control processes to utilize existing capacity.

There is a need to identify acceptable levels of review activity for planning and control purposes. The WVAB plans a 100 per cent check of all DVA declines at the first application and first level of review. A preliminary pilot study of DVA declines on first application indicated an error rate of approximately 2.72%. The current plan to devote 73 per cent of capacity to correct less than 3% of decisions appears excessive. A random sample would provide a measure of the error rate and the department could be required to take appropriate action.

OPTIONS

The study team recommends to the Task Force that the government consider the following:

Status Quo

> As the number of appeals decrease, the Board will devote more resources to reviews. However, the law of diminishing returns will become increasingly operative as administrative costs rise relative to the value of the resulting adjustments. Proposed new service initiatives could be hampered by an inability to take advantage of a reallocation of internal resources.

Phase Down

> One alternative is to develop a long-term plan to gradually phase down the WVAB. It could continue to adjudicate appeals within the current target of 60 days while leaving sufficient resources to hear review-initiated cases based on a sample survey of possible problem areas rather than full scrutiny of all allowance activities undertaken by DVA. A rough estimate is that up to 15 person-years could be saved within three years. Proportional reductions in operating costs would be realized.

Amalgamation

> Amalgamation of the two veterans appeal bodies, the War Veterans Allowance Board (WVAB) and the Pension Review Board (PRB), is feasible. Such a body could be given appeal responsibilities for all programs and services to veterans if an expanded appeal facility was thought appropriate. Such a body would be able to protect the principle of redress, which is fundamental to the veterans program, while enabling the government to provide effective and efficient program delivery in an orderly fashion. The timing of such an amalgamation would need careful consideration.

SECTION 6
LEGAL FRAMEWORK

OBJECTIVE

The legal framework governing the portfolio defines eligibility for benefits, establishes levels for these benefits, defines administrative responsibilities and, to some extent prescribes the processes to be used in benefit deliveries.

AUTHORITY

Appendix A lists the Acts and regulations which provide the authorities for the existence and operations of the department itself, the CPC, the WVAB, the PRB and the BPA. In addition, a number of Orders-in-Council govern the appointments of some officials and the operation of the CPC. With regard to CPC operations, two Orders-in-Council are particularly important: one of 1964 which allows the Governor-in-Council to designate special duty areas and one consolidated in 1981 which actually designates the special duty areas. As matter of interest, the Korean theatre of war is covered by both the latter Order-in-Council and the Veterans Benefits Act, not by the Pension Act as are the two World Wars.

DESCRIPTION

Appendix B lists in four groups the 27 Acts of Parliament which govern the portfolio: those related to pensions, to allowances and grants, to rehabilitation benefits and those dealing with other discrete and related matters.

The existing and legally prescribed pension adjudication process is cumbersome, involving as it does an application, an adjudication thereon and a first appeal to either an Entitlement Board (which may assign an aggravation factor when it makes a favourable decision) or an Assessment Board, or both. For a multitude of reasons at that first level of appeal, an applicant could have to make two

separate and simultaneous submissions: one to the
Entitlement Board and one to the Assessment Board for a
higher assessment.

The PRB is the court of last appeal for pensions in the
portfolio, but their decision can be "set aside" by the
Federal Court which, in such instances, returns the file to
PRB with an outline of deficiencies and a request for
reconsideration.

The Department of Veterans Affairs Act is the legal
authority for the department and authorizes the
Governor-in-Council to approve regulations proposed by the
Minister for a number of purposes and particularly to:

   control and manage various kinds of physical
   installations and institutions;

   prescribe kinds of treatments and training;

   prescribe levels of payments, grants and allowances to
   persons covered by the Act, survivors and dependents;
   and

   make reciprocal arrangements with other countries.

The War Veterans Allowance Act prescribes eligibility
for veterans allowances and the amounts of these allowances;
it also prescribes detailed procedures for quarterly
adjustments of allowances. Bill C-39 was passed in 1984 to
amend the War Veterans Allowance Act, the Civilian War
Pensions and Allowances Act and the Old Age Security Act
with the aim of providing additional benefits for
survivors or dependants and a greater flexibility for
harmonization of benefits with OAS/GIS.

The Acts of Parliament under which the War Veterans
Allowance Board adjudicates are the War Veterans Allowance
Act and the Civilian War Pensions and Allowances Act.

BENEFICIARIES

Canada has an estimated 700,500 veterans and their
survivors or dependants whose eligibility for a disability
pension is governed by the legislative framework and the
related regulations as are the amounts of the pensions.
About 140,000 veterans or their survivors or dependants
receive pensions or were granted lump sums in lieu of a
small pension.

There are approximately 550,000 veterans and their survivors/dependants aged 60 or older. Some 80,000 of these receive allowances.

EXPENDITURES

The current legal framework governs the costs of the benefits authorized and extended, but not the costs related to program delivery (mainly person-year costs). The legal framework thus governed the following 1984/85 expenditures (in millions of dollars):

Disability Pensions	671
Allowances	454
Health Care	180
Land Administration Benefits	2
Special Programs	9
TOTAL	$1,316

OBSERVATIONS

This legal framework has developed over the years to meet needs created by wartime service as they arose. As a result, the framework is a patchwork of laws, Orders-in-Council and regulations and this creates a number of difficulties:

The Canadian Pension Commission

The Pension Act refers to the "Minister" (the Minister of Veterans Affairs or another Minister as may be designated), but does not give particular responsibilities. Rather, it is the Chairman of the Commission who is given the responsibilities and the powers.

Throughout its history, the CPC has generally rendered its decisions with either of three levels of generosity to groups deemed deserving in the following decreasing order: war veterans with service in theatres of war; veterans who have not served in theatres of war; and ex-members of the Canadian Forces who are not veterans. The pertinent Acts are somewhat ambiguous about such differences between degrees of generosity and the CPC has recently been striving to apply to all applicants an equally high degree of generosity. For instance, this has led to CPC decisions and one Federal Court decision which resulted in the granting of a disability pension on the basis of injuries suffered by an

Armed Forces member in non service-related sporting activities, this on the basis that military personnel are required to maintain high standards of physical fitness.

Section 57 of the Pension Act dealing with Exceptional Incapacity is considered ambiguous (Marin report).

The Pension Act covers in some detail the adjudication process. This introduces a great deal of administrative rigidity. As possible solutions, the DVA Pension Process Task Force is examining some 42 suggestions for amendments to the Act. Even if only half of these are adopted, they would require major re-drafting of the Act.

The Pension Act governs a few benefits which are also fully covered in other Acts: last sickness and burial benefits.

The Pension Review Board and the War Veterans Allowance Board

The PRB and the WVAB are governed by separate legislation, but both are required to interpret the law; in particular, the WVAB has made some interpretations which define theatres of war. Being separate, these two boards could differ in their interpretations and in the kinds of precedents they create. The PRB is governed by the legislation without reference to ministerial authority whereas a provision of the War Veterans Allowance Act (Section 30) specifically subjects the WVAB to Ministerial direction (with regard to administration only).

Several cases on which the PRB and the WVAB have adjudicated have been referred to the Federal Court and, in at least two instances, the Court "set aside" cases thus leading to the creation of precedents. The two Boards have also created precedents, particularly in their interpretation of what constitutes theatres of war.

The Pension Review Board does not have to give its reasons for denying an "application to vary" and uses this right in a substantial number of cases to the detriment of those preparing appeals.

Allowances

With regard to veterans allowances, the law is generally interpreted as permitting the Minister to make regulations only on the advice of the War Veterans Allowance Board. This is a most unusual provision which limits the ability of the Minister to fully coordinate the operations of the various elements of his portfolio.

Veterans Land Act

Consideration is being given to amend the Veterans' Land Act in order to enhance recognition of the right ·of spouses in property subject to an agreement of sale.

General

The plethora of Acts of Parliament which govern the granting of benefits to veterans and others, creates a great deal of uncertainty, particularly with regard to marginal cases. As a result, the preparation and support of these cases is lengthy and service to applicants is slower than need be.

Several of the Acts prescribe detailed procedures which limit the margin of manoeuver in adapting to changing circumstances and changing needs of aging veterans. For instance, the Pension Act, the War Veterans Allowance Act, the Civilian War Pensions and Allowances Act, the Compensation for Former Prisoners of War Act and the Veterans Rehabilitation Act include tables of benefits in dollar amounts. In addition, the Pension Act prescribes procedures for first applications and appeals to an Entitlement Board. Usually, such detailed prescriptions are set out in regulations.

OPTIONS

The study team recommends to the Task Force that the Minister of Veterans Affairs consider instructing the Pension Review Board to provide its reasons when denying an "application to vary", and that the government consider authorizing amendments to the legal framework to achieve any or all the following goals:

a. Investing the Minister of Veterans Affairs with the responsibility to administer the Pension Act with regard to his administrative authority over both the CPC and the PRB while leaving them full autonomy in the adjudication process.

b. Ensuring that the law does not permit different interpretations concerning whether or not it authorizes different degrees of generosity based on different kinds of military service.

c. Clarifying the law concerning eligibility of serving members of the Armed Forces for disability pensions arising out of various activities not directly connected with military service.

d. Clarifying Section 57 of the Pension Act (concerning exceptional incapacity) as recommended by the Marin Commission.

e. Ensuring that the pertinent Acts, particularly the Pension Act, do not specify administrative procedures which should more appropriately be the subject of regulations.

f. Eliminating the two current redundancies in law concerning eligibility for benefits.

g. Permitting the amalgamation of the Entitlement and Assessment Boards.

h. Amending the definitions in the legislation, particularly those with regard to theatres of operations (and therefore pertaining to eligibility) so that they are clear and consistent in all the applicable laws.

i. Ensuring that there is no legal restriction concerning the prerogative of the Minister to obtain advice from any source outside the particular element of his portfolio which is primarily concerned.

j. If several of the foregoing proposals for amendments are approved, it would be worth consolidating the Acts listed in the first three categories of Appendix A, thus producing one Act of Parliament with three main sections:

    i) Pensions

        Pension Act
        Civilian War Pensions and Allowances Act
        (also listed in ii), hereunder)

Compensation for Former Prisoners of War Act;
Veterans Benefit Act (also listed in iii),
hereunder).

ii)   Allowances

War Veterans Allowance Act
Women's Royal Naval Services and South
African Military Nursing Service (Benefits)
Act
Allied Veterans Benefits Act
Children of War Dead (Education Assistance)
Act
Civilian War Pensions and Allowances Act
(also listed in i), above)
Supervisors War Service Benefits Act (also
listed in iii), below)
Special Operators War Services Benefits Act
(also listed in iii), below).

iii)   Rehabilitation

Veterans Rehabilitation Act
Reinstatement in Civil Employment Act
Fire Fighters War Service Benefits Act
Veterans Benefit Act (also listed in i),
above)
Supervisors War Service Benefits Act (also
listed in ii), above)
Special Operators War Services Benefits Act
(also listed in ii), above).

APPENDIX A

AUTHORITIES

Department of Veterans Affairs

The department was established by the Department of Veterans Affairs Act (Revised Statutes of Canada 1970, Chapter (c.) V-1 as amended).

The duties, powers and functions of the Minister are set forth in general terms in Section 5 of the Department of Veterans Affairs Act. His authority to make regulations, subject to the approval of the Governor-in-Council, in a number of areas is set out in Section 6. The series of regulations made under the Department of Veterans Affairs Act are as follows:

Assistance Fund (War Veterans Allowances and Civilian War Allowances) Regulations, Consolidated Regulations of Canada (C.R.C.) 1978, c. 1578.
Order-in-Council on agreements with the Canadian National Institute for the Blind for Training and After-care, P.C. 131-4861, dated September 14, 1951, as amended.
Guardianship of Veterans' Property Regulations, C.R.C. 1978, c. 1579.
Last Post Fund Regulations, C.R.C. 1978, c. 1580.
Pensioners Training Regulations, C.R.C. 1978, c. 1581.
Veterans Burial Regulations, C.R.C. 1978, c. 1583, as amended.
Veterans Care Regulations, 1984-635 (SOR).
Veterans Estates Regulations, C.R.C. 1978, c. 1584.
Vetcraft Shops Regulations, C.R.C. 1978, c. 1582.
Veterans Treatment Regulations, C.R.C. 1978, c. 1585, as amended.

The other statutes administered by the department under the direction of the Minister are as follows:

Allied Veterans Benefits Act, R.S.C. 1952, c. 8.
Children of War Dead (Education Assistance) Act, R.S.C. 1970, c. C-18, as amended.
Children of War Dead (Education Assistance) Regulations, C.R.C. 1978, c. 399.

Fire Fighters War Service Benefits Act, R.S.C. 1952,
  c. 117.
The Returned Soldiers' Insurance Act, S.C. 1920, c. 54,
  as amended.
Returned Soldiers' Insurance Regulations, C.R.C. 1978,
  c. 1390.
Soldier Settlement Act, R.S.C. 1927, c. 188, as
  amended.
Special Operators War Service Benefits Act, R.S.C.
  1952, c. 256.
Supervisors War Service Benefits Act, R.S.C. 1952, c.
  258.
Veterans Benefit Act, R.S.C. 1970, c. V-2, as amended.
Veterans Insurance Act, R.S.C. 1970, c. V-3, as
  amended.
Veterans Insurance Regulations, C.R.C. 1978, c. 1587.
Veterans' Land Act, R.S.C. 1970, c. V-4, as amended.
Veterans' Land Regulations, C.R.C. 1978, c. 1594, as
  amended.
Regional Advisory Committee Regulations, C.R.C. 1978,
  c. 1593.
Veterans Rehabilitation Act, R.S.C. 1970, c. V-5.
Veterans Rehabilitation Regulations, C.R.C. 1978, c.
  1595.
War Service Grants Act, R.S.C. 1970, c. W-4.
War Service Grants Regulations, C.R.C. 1978, c. 1601.
Women's Royal Naval Services and the South African
  Military Nursing Service (Benefits) Act, R.S.C. 1952,
  c. 297.

Canadian Pension Commission

The statutes administered by the Canadian Pension
Commission are as follows:

Pension Act, R.S.C. 1970, c. P-7, as amended.
Civilian War Pensions and Allowances Act (Parts I to
  X), R.S.C. 1970, c. C-20, as amended.
The Compensation for Former Prisoners of War Act, S.C.
  1974-75-76, c. 95, as amended.
The Halifax Relief Commission Pension Continuation Act,
  S.C. 1974-75-76, c. 88, as amended.

The Commission also adjudicates or makes
recommendations on claims under the following:

The Flying Accidents Compensation Regulations, C.R.C.
  1978, c. 10, as amended.

Supplementary Pensions under the Women's Royal Naval
    Services and the South African Military Nursing
    Services (Benefits) Act, R.S.C. 1952, c. 297.
The Special Operators War Service Benefits Act, R.S.C.
    1952, c. 256.
The Royal Canadian Mounted Police Superannuation Act,
    R.S.C. 1970, c. R-11, as amended.
The Royal Canadian Mounted Police Pension Continuation
    Act, R.S.C. 1970, c. R-10 as amended.
The Gallantry Gratuities and Annuities Order, P.C.
    1974-723, dated March 26, 1974.
Penitentiary Inmates Accident Compensation Regulations,
    P.C. 1982-1026, dated April 1, 1982.
Special Indemnity Plan for Dependants of Canadian
    Forces Attachés, T.B. 753619, dated December 1, 1977.
The Defence Services Pension Continuation Act, R.S.C.
    1970, c. D-3 as amended.

War Veterans Allowance Board

The legislation under which the Board adjudicates is as
follows:

War Veterans Allowance Act, R.S.C. 1970, c. W-5, as
    amended.
Veterans Allowance Regulations, C.R.C. 1978, c. 1602,
    as amended.
Part XI, Civilian War Pensions and Allowances Act,
    R.S.C. 1970, c. C-20, as amended.
Civilian Allowances Regulations, C.R.C. 1978, c. 402,
    as amended.

Pension Review Board

Pension Act, R.S.C. 1970, c. P-7, as amended (Sections
    75 to 81).

Bureau of Pensions Advocates

Pension Act, R.S.C. 1970, c. P-7, as amended (Part II).

POSSIBLE GROUPING OF THE RELEVANT ACTS OF PARLIAMENT

Twenty-seven Acts of Parliament and several Orders-in-Council constitute the legal framework for the granting of benefits to veterans, to certain categories of civilians who served in wartime and, subject to certain conditions, to their dependants and their survivors.

The pertinent Acts and Orders-in-Council can be grouped in the following categories:

a. Those related to pensions:

1. Pension Act
2. Civilian War Pensions and Allowances Act (also listed in sub-paragraph b), hereunder)
3. Compensation for Former Prisoners of War Act
4. Veterans Benefit Act (also listed in sub-paragraph c), hereunder).

b. Those related to allowances and grants:

1. War Veterans Allowance Act
2. Women's Royal Naval Services and South African Military Nursing Service (Benefits) Act
3. Allied Veterans Benefits Act
4. Children of War Dead (Education Assistance) Act
5. Civilian War Pensions and Allowances Act (also listed in sub-paragraph a), above)
6. Supervisors War Service Benefits Act (also listed in sub-paragraph c), below)
7. Special Operators War Services Benefits Act (also listed in sub-paragraph c), below).

c. Those related to rehabilitation benefits:

1. Veterans Rehabilitation Act
2. Reinstatement in Civil Employment Act
3. Fire Fighters War Service Benefits Act
4. Veterans Benefit Act (also listed in sub-paragraph a), above)
5. Supervisors War Service Benefits Act
6. Special Operators War Services Benefits Act.

d.   Others dealing with related but discrete matters (some no longer authorize new benefits):

1.   RCMP Superannuation Act
2.   RCMP Pension Continuation Act
3.   Gallantry Gratuities (Order-in-Council)
4.   Halifax Relief Commission Pension Continuation Act
5.   Department of Veterans Affairs Act
6.   Army Benevolent Fund Act
7.   Defence Services Pension Continuation Act
8.   National Defence Act
9.   Veterans' Land Act (will become redundant in a few years)
10. Returned Soldiers' Insurance Act
11. Soldiers Settlement Act
12. Veterans' Business and Professional Loans Act
13. War Service Grants Act
14. Veterans Insurance Act.

SECTION 7
OVERLAP WITH OTHER FEDERAL/PROVINCIAL
PROGRAMS OR PRIVATE SECTOR SERVICES

Summary and Overview

General

This section reviews the programs and/or services provided by the Veterans Affairs portfolio in terms of those where an equivalent or similar program or service exists in another part of the federal government, in a provincial government or in the private sector. There appear to be five such programs/services in the portfolio as follows:

Old Age Security/Guaranteed Income Supplement which provides income support to all citizens, including veterans, over 65 years of age.

Health Services available from the provincial medicare plans which are duplicated by the Ste-Anne's Hospital and two veterans' homes.

The routine medical examinations of the Canadian Pension Commission.

The dental services provided by the DVA Dental Clinics.

The Aging Veterans Program which provides services such as home and institutional care which are also provided by provincial governments' seniors' programs.

Four of these areas are discussed in detail in this section. In the paragraphs which follow, they are summarized and the Health Services overlap is also discussed.

Harmonization of Veterans Allowances with OAS/GIS Benefits

As the beneficiaries of veterans' allowances reach 65 years of age or widows/widowers in receipt of spousal allowances reach 60 years of age, they become eligible for the OAS/GIS benefits available to all Canadians. However, OAS/GIS benefits are slightly lower than the allowances and a "topping up" of up to $1,000 per year occurs. Currently, income definitions differ between GIS and the allowances so that DVA must apply a parallel income test to that applied by the Department of Health and Welfare (i.e. the veteran must apply separately to each department for the GIS and the allowance). Efforts to "harmonize" these two income tests are aimed at making them as identical as possible so that one application would suffice and only one administrative cost would be incurred.

Seven methods of "harmonization" have been examined. All would improve the administration but some would significantly increase the cost of allowances. The department is planning to streamline the existing payment system and to implement a partial harmonization (Appendix 1) which should save about 170 person-years without increasing the allowances. In our opinion, closer harmonization could be readily achieved by implementing two of the other options for an additional 20 to 40 person-years saving in administrative costs with no increase in the allowance costs.

Health Services Available from Provincial Health Plans

The department used to have some 13 hospitals and a number of veterans' homes situated across the country. In 1963, the department commenced negotiations with the provinces to arrange the transfer of the hospitals to provincial jurisdiction. In return, the department arranged to have access to a number of contract beds on a priority basis. The first hospital was transferred in 1966 and by 1983 all but one, Ste.Anne's in Montreal, had been transferred. As well, two veterans' homes are still operated by the department.

At the present time, the department's institutions provide 1,305 beds and some 4,900 beds are available on contract where the department only has to "top-up" the provincial obligation to the veteran as a senior citizen. The cost of the department's 1,305 beds is about $53 million per year whereas the 4,900 contract beds cost $66 million per year plus a capital transfer cost that averaged $33 million per year during the past three years (i.e. the contract beds, because of the "top-up" arrangement even with the capital transfer cost which will eventually terminate, are less than half of the cost of the department's own beds). However, if the hospital and two veterans' homes were transferred to the two provinces concerned, only about half of the present patients would be eligible for the "top-up" contract rate (i.e. the department would have to pay about $40,000 a bed per year for the other half of the beds).

The net effect would be that the annual cost would be reduced from $53 million to $33 million offset by the capital transfer cost which could be in the range of $50 million to $100 million based on previous arrangements. In other words, the department could recover the capital transfer costs in three to four years.

CPC Medical Examinations

The Canadian Pension Commission carries out some 18,360 medical examinations a year. About 7,900 of these are as a result of first applications for pensions or successful appeals or a request by a pensioner. The remaining 10,460 are carried out routinely as a service to pensioners to detect any change in the pensioned condition. About one-third of these routine examinations lead to an increase in the pension.

The cost of a CPC medical examination is about $230 compared to a typical provincial medicare cost of $30 to $60. Those 6,974 routine examinations which did not result in an increase in assessment cost an estimated $1,595,170. If all the 10,460 routine examinations were first carried out by private sector doctors and a questionnaire completed, then the CPC medical examiners would need to see only about 3,860 persons of whom the status would have changed for 3,486. This would make some 28 person-years and $1,511,820 available for reallocation if the cost of the private sector medical examinations were paid by provincial medicare or $988,000 if it were paid by the Canadian Pension Commission.

Dental Clinics

The Department of Veterans Affairs currently spends about $9 million on dental services. Of this amount, about $3 million (and 69 person-years) represents the cost of operating some 16 Dental Clinics across the country and the remainder is spent on the "Dentist of Choice" program. The department makes its dental services available to other government departments on a cost recovery basis. It is estimated that $4 million or 44% of expenditures are recovered in this way. Currently, 14,000 cases a year are treated in the Dental Clinics and 28,000 cases a year are treated by private sector dentists; the cost per case is about the same. However, of the 14,000 cases treated by the Dental Clinics, 3,500 or 25% were for members of the RCMP, students under the auspices of CIDA, Canada Council award holders, CUSO field staff returning from foreign assignments, etc. (Note that the RCMP account for 98% of the usage by non-veterans.) It is suggested that the department reconsider its position regarding operation of Dental Clinics. Purchasing more of such services from the private sector would allow up to 60 person-years to be redeployed.

Provincial Seniors Programs

The department's Aging Veterans Program provides services such as home and institutional care to selected categories of veterans over 65 years of age. Many of the provinces also provide such services and veterans are often eligible for these as well.

However, as this section shows, the provincial programs vary greatly from province to province. In general, the Atlantic provinces have very little in the way of special programs for senior citizens whereas the central and western provinces all have some type of program. The Aging Veterans Program is designed to complement the provincial programs and to bring the services provided up to a uniform single national standard for all veterans. The provincial contribution to the "home" care program was estimated in section 3 as $16 million versus the department's cost of $5 million. It would appear that the department is being successful in ensuring that its AVP benefits complement, and do not duplicate, those available from the provinces.

Harmonization of Veterans Allowances
with OAS/GIS Benefits

OBJECTIVE

To "harmonize" veterans' allowances and OAS/GIS benefits to the extent possible; (i.e. to minimize differences in the way incomes are calculated for GIS and veterans' allowances purposes).

AUTHORITY

Veterans' allowances are governed by War Veterans Allowance Act (as amended by Bill C-39 of June 1984); and Civilian War Pensions and Allowances Act.

DESCRIPTION

As the beneficiaries of veterans' allowances reach age 65 and widows or widowers in receipt of spousal allowances reach age 60, they become eligible for the OAS/GIS benefits available to all Canadians. OAS/GIS benefits are not as great as the amount set for veterans' allowance beneficiaries and the department provides a "topping-up". For instance, a single veteran (non-blind) receiving OAS and GIS can receive up to $670 per year in veterans' allowances.

Currently, income definitions for veterans' allowances and GIS are different; moreover, the former is based on current income, whereas the latter is calculated on the previous year's income. Harmonization efforts are intended to narrow the differences between the two sets of rules to the extent possible. Even after this degree of harmonization, however, it is expected that some differences will remain:

    a.   veterans will still be required to apply to two departments, DVA and NHW; and

    b.   both these departments will continue to use their own income test parameters.

Bill C-39 which amends the War Veterans Allowance Act was passed in June 1984 to permit harmonization, inter alia, by adopting major features of the GIS income test, including definition of income, payment and accounting years.

BENEFICIARIES

The beneficiaries are recipients of veterans' allowances aged 65 or older and their widows/widowers aged 60 to 64 in receipt of spousal allowances. They numbered about 49,000 on March 31, 1985, out of a total of some 362,000 veterans and widows/widowers in that age group. The number in that group is expected to peak at approximately 460,000 in 1991 and, if the percentage of those eligible for allowances remains the same (13.5%), some 62,000 beneficiaries will then receive allowances. With the passage of time, survivors become an increasing percentage of this group of beneficiaries.

EXPENDITURES

A total of 440 PYs in the head office, regional and district office administer and deliver the allowances to the beneficiaries.

OBSERVATIONS

NHW obtains income data from Revenue Canada (Taxation) through compatible tapes. DVA will develop tapes compatible with those of NHW.

Appendix 1 sets out two series of harmonization options: Series A which would retain the current sliding scale of allowances and Series B which are flat rate allowance options.

Option A.1 in the Appendix describes current harmonization plans which are expected to save up to 170 PYs. Measures described in options A.2 and A.3 would permit further savings of some 40 PYs. Of themselves, these options would not make appreciable changes in the total amount spent on allowances.

Options A.4 and A.5 would not produce appreciable additional PY savings, but they would generate large increases in the total amount spent on allowances.

Option B.1 would be a flat rate allowance tied to current DVA income parameters. It would not generate appreciable changes in the total amount spent on allowances and would permit savings of some 70 to 90 PYs in addition to the streamlining savings of option A.1 for a total of 170 to 190 PYs.

140

Options B.2 and B.3 would be tied to GIS income parameters. They would open eligibility to a larger number of applicants and would increase substantially the amount spent on allowances, this without appreciable PY savings above those of option B.1.

Options B.1, B.2 and B.3 would be averages: depending on the level selected some current beneficiaries would receive slightly more and others slightly less than they now receive. This could give rise to perceived inequities.

It is clear, therefore, that the flat rate options would not yield additional PY savings and would create one of two difficulties: perceived inequities or a large increase in the amount of allowances paid.

OPTIONS

The study team recommends to the Task Force that the government consider the following harmonization alternatives for DVA:

a.   Implementing the currently planned measures to harmonize the allowance program with OAS/GIS (Appendix A, A.1) to yield some 170 PYs for re-allocation without increasing the total amount spent on allowances.

b.   In addition to the foregoing, extending harmonization to include options A.2 and A.3 (Appendix 1) to yield an additional 20 to 40 PYs for re-allocation to a possible total of 210 without increasing the total amount spent on allowances.

OPTIONS REGARDING THE ALLOWANCE PROGRAM

OPTION	COMMENTS REGARDING OPTION	CHANGE IN EXPENDITURES FOR ALLOWANCES	PERSON YEAR REQUIREMENTS
A.1 Partial harmonization with GIS.	Currently being implemented. Includes streamlining procedures. Harmonization adopts the following GIS features: mail-in approach; adjudication and benefit control; payment and accounting year; automatic benefit calculation; automatic renewal process. Minimal impact on allowance recipients. Implementation involves transferring information by computer tape from NHW to DVA for single veterans receiving OAS/GIS and married veterans where both husband and wife are receiving OAS/GIS. The tape would provide information on about 37,000 of the 87,000 recipients.	Negligible.	• Currently require about 440 P-Ys. • Streamlining procedures will save 100 P-Ys. • Harmonization will save 40-70 P-Ys. • Net P-Y requirement is 270-300.
A.2 Partial harmonization with GIS but with extended tape transfer.	Same as option A.1 but include the following allowance recipients on the tape transferred from NHW to DVA: surviving spouse receiving OAS/GIS and married veterans whose spouse is receiving an OAS/GIS equivalent from NHW. Option A.2 would include the more complex cases compared to option A.1. It would pick up information on an additional 12,000 recipients. This option would become more significant as the age of the veteran population increases.	Negligible.	• Save an additional 13-23 P-Ys. • Net P-Y requirement is 250-290.
A.3 More complete harmonization with GIS.	Same as options A.1 and A.2 but also adopt the GIS feature of reacting only to permanent income changes. Small short-term impact on recipients; negligible longer-term impact.	Negligible.	• Save an additional 10-20 P-Ys. • Net P-Y requirement is 230-280.
A.4 Yet more complete harmonization with GIS.	Same as options A.1-A.3 but also adopt the GIS feature of exempting disability pensions, family allowances, interest and casual earnings. Recipients' allowance payments would increase.	Increase expenditures by $25-30 million over current level.	Negligible additional P-y savings.
A.5 Complete harmonization with GIS.	Same as options A.1-A.4 but also adopt the GIS feature of deducting only $1.00 for every 2.00 of assessable income. Recipients' allowance payments would increase.	Increase expenditures by $30-40 million over current level.	Negligible additional P-y savings.
B.1 Flat rate allowance that is tied to WVA eligibility for veterans aged 65 or over.	Includes streamlining procedures. Could adopt selected GIS features for allowance recipients under 65 but this would not result in P-y savings in addition to those identified in A1. P-y savings would accrue from flat rate allowance paid to recipients 65 and over. Allowances for recipients 65 and over could be paid by NHW. Some recipients would lose and others would gain.	Negligible.	• Currently require about 440 P-Ys. • Streamlining procedures will save 100 P-Ys. • Flat rate allowance would save 70-90 P-Ys. • Net P-Y requirement is 250-270.
B.2 Flat rate allowance that is tied to GIS eligibility.	Similar to option B.1 except tied to GIS rather than WVA eligibility.	Increase expenditures by about $50 million over current level.	Same as for option B.1.
B.3 Flat rate allowance tied to GIS amount.	As GIS mounts decrease, the allowance would also decrease in accordance with a fixed schedule.	Increase expenditures by about $30-40 million over current year.	Approximately the same as for option B.1.

Reduction in the Number of
CPC Medical Examinations

OBJECTIVE

The purposes of the CPC medical examinations are to assess the bases of requests for disability pensions and to provide medical follow-up for disability pensioners.

AUTHORITY

CPC medical examinations are authorized and, in some instances, required by the Pension Act.

DESCRIPTION

For 1984/85, the CPC had planned the following medical support activities and the actual performance turned out to be close (in fact slightly higher with a slightly greater PY utilization):

Activities	Output	PYs Utilized
Management	-	4.0
Medical examinations	18,360	20.4
Field medical reviews	23,000	3.5
Field medical opinions	1,600	1.6
Head Office medical opinions	9,275	9.2
Head Office medical reviews*	4,800	4.5
Field medical reports	18,360	109.3
Medical Reviews typed	13,800	12.0
Medical Decisions promulgated	29,600	15.9

The activities which employ large numbers of PYs are the medical examinations and the preparation of the reports. Some 7,900 of these 18,360 examinations were carried out at the request of applicants and pensioners or resulted from CPC and PRB decisions; they are therefore considered non-discretionary. The remainder, 10,460, were carried out as follow-up and were therefore at the discretion of the CPC; this follow-up is on the basis of re-examination dates set at the last examination and questionnaires sent to and filled out by the pensioners.

* Including quality control.

The CPC plans to gradually increase the number of medical examinations per year to 25,000 in 1988/89, increasing proportionately the PY requirement. It is recognized, however, that the available resources may prevent reaching this goal.

The 109.3 PYs listed against field medical reports actually carried out various functions as follows:

a. 38 PYs for management, administration and counselling;

b. 29 PYs for office reception, clerical duties and ancillary benefits; and

c. 42 PYs in duties directly connected with the medical examinations, i.e., medical report typing, making medical appointments, filing, preparing documentation.

BENEFICIARIES

New applicants for disability pensions (4,429 in 1984) and the disability pensioners (approximately 100,000) are the beneficiaries of the CPC medical examinations.

EXPENDITURES

Of the activities and PYs listed above, the following were directly related to the pension medical examinations:

Activities	PYs
Management	4
Medical Examinations	20.4
Head Office Medical Opinions	9.2
Head Office Medical Reviews	4.5
Field Medical Reports	42
	80.1

Including the contributions to employee benefit plans, these PYs cost $3,562,500. In addition, $637,000 was spent for contract physicians and specialist referrals.

OBSERVATIONS

In 1984-85, approximately one-third of the 10,460 discretionary examinations resulted in a change of pension so that some 6,974 medical examinations turned out to be non-essential for pension purposes.

It would be possible for the CPC medical examiners to make better use of questionnaires regarding present health status by having pensioners take them to their personal physicians when the proposed examinations are discretionary. Decisions to call in pensioners for an examination by a Pension Examiner would be made on the basis of these questionnaires when it appears that changes have occurred.

Although some personal physicians may charge to fill out a questionnaire, it can be assumed that such an approach would not significantly increase medicare costs; the pensioners who, by definition, have some kind of disability, are likely to see their personal physicians on a regular basis. In any case, medicare pays for one physical examination per year. On receipt of the completed questionnaire, the pension examiner would decide whether or not to examine the individual.

Assuming an "over-insurance" of 10%, this approach should allow a reduction of some 6600 medical examinations (based on the 1984/85 workload). This would be a reduction of about 36% in the workload of medical examinations and examination report typing; it is therefore estimated that some 28 PYs (costing $1,282,500) would be available for re-allocation and $229,320 in physician and specialist fees could be saved.

OPTIONS

The study team recommends to the Task Force that the government consider the following options:

> the CPC continue to carry out medical examinations at the current rate of 18,360;

> the CPC increase the yearly number of medical examinations to 25,000 by 1988/89, as planned;

> the CPC schedule only the non-discretionary medical examinations, depending on personal physicians to indicate whether or not a follow up medical examination of a pensioner is warranted.

Dental Clinics

OBJECTIVE

To provide free dental services to veterans who would be eligible by reason of receiving WVA/CWA allowances, being in receipt of a CPC pension for a specified disability where dental treatment is required, or being a veteran occupying a bed in the institutional or domiciliary care category.

AUTHORITY

The Department of Veterans Affairs Act provides that the department can offer dental services as part of its health care programs.

BENEFICIARIES

Based on projections made in a departmental evaluation report dated December 1982, some 68,000 veterans are eligible to use the dental services. It is estimated that less than one-third do so.

EXPENDITURES

The dental services program has a budget of about $9 million and 92 person-years. However, some $4 million is recovered from other users such as the RCMP for a net cost of about $5 million.

DESCRIPTION

The function of the dental services program is patient care. Eligible veterans are entitled to "basic" dental treatment only. The service is not for cosmetic dentistry such as crowns and bridges unless it is essential for the dental health of the patient. Other users have their own rules as to what services may be provided. These users include the RCMP, students under the auspices of CIDA, Canada Council award holders, candidates of CUSO returning from foreign assignments and some others referred by government departments. The RCMP account for about 98% of the other users. As well, where there is a provincial denticare plan under which the veteran is eligible for free dental services, then the veteran is directed to use the provincial plan instead of the department's plan.

The dental services program is offered through the 16 departmental dental clinics and a "Dentist of Choice" program. Service volume is measured by case which may represent a series of appointments for one patient. In fact, the departmental clinics average three appointments per case for veterans. The table below indicates the number of cases for veterans and for other users for each part of the program (based on 1981/82 figures).

	Department Clinics	Dentist of Choice	Total
Veterans	10,600	11,900	22,500
Other Users	3,700	16,000	19,700
TOTAL	14,300	27,900	42,200

OBSERVATIONS

The cost per case for the "Dentist of Choice" and the Departmental Dental Clinic is about the same at $230.

As the veterans age, it will be increasingly difficult for them to access the departmental dental clinics. The "Dentist of Choice" program should always be able to locate a dentist close to the veteran's home.

There appears to be a need for special geriatric dentistry which is not being met by the private sector. A small number of the departmental dental clinics could probably economically specialize in this area.

The volume of veterans eligible for dental services will decline steadily over the next 10 years. A number of the 16 clinics will probably become uneconomic each year. It should be possible to determine the economic number of cases needed to justify a clinic. Those clinics with an insufficient number of cases could be closed.

The provision of dental services to the RCMP and others now represents 44% of the budget. Despite the fact that the department is reimbursed for these services, it is very questionable that the department should continue to provide them at this level when they are available directly from the private sector.

OPTIONS

The study team recommends to the Task Force that the government consider the following options:

the department to continue with the present arrangements adjusting the level of services to the demand;

the department to terminate its operation of dental clinics and particularly with regard to providing dental services to other users such as the RCMP.

Provincial Seniors Programs

OBJECTIVE

To assess and, when possible, make use of the provincial senior citizens programs for veterans.

AUTHORITY

All benefits discussed herein are under provincial jurisdiction.

DESCRIPTION

Newfoundland has very little in the way of benefits for the aged. Veterans who are welfare cases are considered a federal responsibility and are referred to DVA.

Nova Scotia benefits for senior citizens are limited to medical assessments of welfare cases to determine whether nursing home placement is necessary. Costs of health care services are largely borne by private sources.

Prince Edward Island resources are limited as are benefits to the aged. These are mainly social and medical assessments leading to health care provided by private persons or organizations. These services amount to less than Aging Veterans Program (AVP) contributions. A user fee geared to income is levied.

New Brunswick provides limited services to the aged, but only in urban centres. These services involve assessments and follow-up.

Québec has a very limited budget for social and medical programs. The province provides a comprehensive assessment as does the AVP, but has a long waiting list for health care. Since only the most needy can receive services, veterans get more immediate attention from DVA which also provides a better range of services.

Ontario provides a broad spectrum of benefits generally similar to those of the AVP (but less complete). Costs are covered by OHIP when prescribed by a physician; otherwise, there is a user fee geared to income. Services are good and coordinated in urban areas but incomplete in rural areas. The AVP "tops-up" provincial benefits.

Manitoba provides an AVP-type assessment which is, however, more limited than the AVP. Follow-up is spotty, particularly in rural areas. Residents of the province pay co-insurance premiums. Long term care is subject to a user fee.

Saskatchewan has a limited and spotty program centered on urban areas. Residents of the province pay co-insurance premiums and user fees for long term care.

Alberta provides limited assistance through several programs. It is intended to move toward a "single entry" and more global assessment process.

British Columbia provides fairly complete AVP-type assessments and services. These are supplemented by community-based programs requiring user fees; when clients cannot pay, the provincial department of human resources assists to the degree possible. AVP is a "top-up".

BENEFICIARIES

The beneficiaries of the provincial health care programs are citizens of the provinces aged 65 or older and, in some circumstances, younger citizens with acute needs.

EXPENDITURES

The expenditures are covered in various ways in provincial budgets.

OBSERVATIONS

DVA has examined in some depth the existing provincial health care programs. It is clear that no province can take over AVP-like responsibilities for its resident veterans and provide services that would be equal in variety and quality, even with repayment from DVA.

Notwithstanding the foregoing, DVA ensures that all available and suitable provincial benefits are exhausted before AVP benefits are granted. In those cases, AVP benefits are a "top-up".

Finally, the good follow-up in the AVP program (monitoring the extent to which authorized benefits are actually being used) cannot be taken over by any province.

OPTIONS

The study team considers the current AVP and the continuing efforts to use available provincial benefits the best approach. This program should be expanded where possible and as required.

SECTION 8
VETERANS LAND ADMINISTRATION (VLA)

OBJECTIVE

To provide financial assistance by way of loans and grants for the purchase of property and improvements to help qualified veterans settle in Canada.

AUTHORITY

Veterans' Land Act and its regulations.

DESCRIPTION

VLA assists veterans, their heirs, devisees or personal representatives to manage and acquire title to the property on which the veterans are established. As of March 1975, new loans ceased although veterans with existing loans could apply for additional ones until March 1977.

As of March 1985, there were approximately 27,000 properties registered under the name of the Director, VLA which represent a total indebtedness of $200 million. All loans will have matured by 2007.

Lands Administration is organized into three principal areas. Property and Estates processes the documentation accompanying the transfer of land from the Director to the veteran or his/her beneficiary, in case of death, when the loan has been repaid. Other functions include preparing documentation for releases of portions of land, partial sales, easements, leases, etc. Fund Accounting involves the collection of all payments due to the Crown on the outstanding agreements. Field Operations counsels veterans, appraises properties and provides a variety of property management services to veterans.

Average turnaround time from the veteran's request for transfer documents to their receipt is 21 days; for work coming into head office, the turnaround time is between 3 to 4 days. Goals for arrears of account payments, unresolved estate cases, preparation for centralization, human resource planning, advice to the Minister and official language usage are negotiated annually and often exceeded. A recent client survey found much satisfaction with VLA in the veteran community.

A three-year plan to centralize the fund accounting and property management processes and phase out the four regional offices is being implemented. A reduction of 55 PYs in regional positions (during 1985/86 to 1988/89) is antici-pated with an increase in 13 positions at VLA, Charlottetown for a net reduction of 42 PYs.

On a national basis, field officers are on the road approximately 50 per cent of the time. The remainder of the time is devoted to seeing clients in the office, conducting business over the telephone and preparing reports. Visits are arranged on the basis of an essential requirement to see the client or the property. Other clients in the area would be visited to make up a full day. When centralization is complete, field and district personnel will make up 58 percent of total person-years for the program.

BENEFICIARIES

A total of 143,000 veterans have been assisted under the Veterans' Land Act.

EXPENDITURES

The approved budget for 1985-86 for the management of property contracts under the Veterans' Land Act is $6 million and 183 PYs.

OBSERVATIONS

Collocation with Veterans Services, DVA, occurs in approximately 70 percent of locations. The thrust is towards collocation where accommodation space is available. However, management, administrative and support services are provided by VLA personnel. However, the next two years may see an increase in repayment rates due to the number of clients who reach retirement age and who earn their grant.

The consolidation of decision-making and operational functions at headquarters recognizes the need to wind down the program in response to the declining number of clients and loans outstanding. However, the next two years may see an increase in repayment rates due to the number of clients who reach retirement age and who earn their grant.

There is a certain amount of discretionary work at the field office level. This is estimated at approximately 25 per cent.

154

Level of service of the program is high as evidenced by a three-week turnaround of document requests and the comprehensive nature of the counselling and property management services offered upon request by VLA field officers.

OPTIONS

The study team recommends to the Task Force that the government consider:

continuing the centralization of operations as planned with a review in several years for further resource reductions;

accelerating the centralization process now planned to occur over three years to take place, instead, over 18-24 months. This would likely result in quicker service to the client but it may necessitate the layoff of staff close to retirement age;

achieving resource savings through modifications in the level of service. Service levels in all areas may be sufficiently high to permit resource savings targeted at up to an additional 30 P-Ys. These savings could come from the district level and headquarters and include both operations and administration;

contracting out property management functions to the private sector where feasible and cost effective. Some suggested areas may be property management services to veterans and preparation of legal documents;

amalgamating VLA functions into Veterans Services, DVA. This would lower overhead costs in the area of management, administration and support services.

SECTION 9
COMMONWEALTH WAR GRAVES COMMISSION

OBJECTIVE

The Commonwealth War Graves Commission marks and maintains the graves of the members of the Forces of the Commonwealth and Empire who died in the two world wars, builds memorials to the dead whose graves are unknown and keeps records and registers. Costs are shared by partner governments.

AUTHORITY

The Commonwealth War Graves Commission was established by Royal Charter of May 21, 1917, the provisions of which were amended and extended by a Supplemental Charter of June 8, 1964.

The Appropriation Authority for Canada's share of the costs is Vote 5, Grants and Contributions, Veterans Affairs Program.

DESCRIPTION

The Commission operates in 140 countries commemorating 1,694,813 Commonwealth war dead of the two World Wars. Canadian war dead number about 110,000 and are buried in 74 of those countries.

The full cost of the work is shared by the partner governments - the United Kingdom, Canada, Australia, New Zealand, South Africa and India - in the proportion of the numbers of their war graves.

The Commission is composed of a President (H.R.H. The Duke of Kent), the High Commissioners resident in London of the participating governments, the South African Ambassador in London and 12 others appointed by Her Majesty The Queen.

By an Instrument executed under the Royal Charter, the Minister of Veterans Affairs is the Commission's Canadian Agent. A Secretary-General of the Canadian Agency is appointed by the Commission and is responsible for the operations of the Commission in Canada and the United States.

BENEFICIARIES

Families, relatives and friends of the 1.7 million Commonwealth war dead of the two World Wars; and Canadian people in honouring their debt to those who died.

EXPENDITURES

Canada's contribution in 1983/84 was $2,018,818. This represented 9.88 per cent of the total cost of operation of the Commission. The main estimates for 1984/85 and 1985/86 are $2.5 million.

OBSERVATIONS

Investigation by the team was limited to a visit of the Canadian Agency in Ottawa which consists of a Secretary General and three staff. It appears to be operating in a reasonably efficient and effective mode.

OPTIONS

The study team recommends to the Task Force that the government consider that since the level of Canada's grant is established by the proportion of Canadian war graves, the only alternative to the current grant would appear to be withdrawal from the organization. There appears to be no reason to consider this option.

SECTION 10
UNITED STATES VETERANS ADMINISTRATION

By way of comparison, the following paragraphs describe the organization of the U.S. Veterans Administration which is responsible to:

a. ensure that medical care is provided on a timely basis within the law to all authorized veterans;

b. ensure that an appropriate level of benefits is provided within the law to eligible veterans and beneficiaries;

c. ensure that the memorial affairs of eligible veterans are appropriately provided for and conducted in a dignified manner which recognizes the honorable status of veterans; and

d. serve as the leader within the U.S. federal government on all matters directly affecting veterans and their families and be their advocate in representing their just needs.

AUTHORITY

The Veterans Administration was established by the President in 1930 to bring together several previous agencies dating as far back as the Revolutionary War.

DESCRIPTION

The benefits include compensation payments for disabilities or death related to military service; pensions based on financial need for totally disabled veterans or certain survivors for disabilities or death not related to military service; education and rehabilitation; home loan guaranties; burial, including cemeteries, markers, flags, etc.; and a comprehensive medical program involving a widespread system of nursing homes, clinics, and more than 170 medical centres.

The program consists of the following major elements:

a. Compensation for Service-connected disability (disability pension from 10% to 100% by increments of 10%). There is no means test. Serving personnel cannot receive this compensation while serving.

b.   Dependancy and Indemnity Compensation to survivors (active duty or service-connected deaths).
c.   Disability pension, non-service connected disability. Past age 65, all veterans are deemed to have some degree of disability, and this "disability" pension is subject to a means test (based on the applicants own statements; the IRS will not provide this information).
d.   Death pension to survivors, non service-connected.
e.   Burial Benefits.
f.   Education assistance (including dependants).
g.   Loan guaranties.
h.   Life Insurance.

Veterans receiving a military compensation of pension cannot also have a veteran's compensation or pension for disability. Since the military pension is non-contributory, this would be seen as double-dipping. There is always some legislation being proposed to change this, but the proposal is generally seen as unlikely to succeed.

Most States and even some counties offer special concessions to veterans (e.g., waiving property taxes).

A separate Board of Veterans Appeals reports directly to the Administrator. This is the final appeal body, but a veteran can renew an appeal at any time, on the basis of new facts coming to light (including new advances in medicine). This Board entertains appeals related to all the various kinds of veterans benefits.

BENEFICIARIES

There is a total veteran population of 28.5M, of whom 7M receive benefits. The aging of the veteran population is seen as a looming problem of enormous dimensions: there are now 3.3M veterans over age 65 and there will be 12M by 2010 A.D. This could become very expensive in medical costs.

There is no compensation for ex-PoWs as such, but 38% of them receive some Veteran Administration benefits, vice 7% for the overall veteran population.

EXPENDITURES

In 1983, the U.S. Veterans Administration had budgeted:

a.	Compensation and Pensions	$15.9B
b.	Medical Care	7.7B
c.	General Operating Expenses	0.69B
d.	Construction	0.8B
e.	Funds and Grants	3.7B
	TOTAL	$28.9B

OBSERVATIONS

The Administrator sits on the Cabinet Council (comparable to an outer Cabinet) but reports directly to the President. Several Congressional committees monitor the activities of the Administration - each year they have a first review of the proposed Administration budget.

A number of veterans associations monitor the activities of the Administration (the American Legion, American Vets, Paralysed Vets, PoW associations, etc).

The Veterans Administration does not have the equivalent of a Bureau of Pensions Advocates but relies on veterans associations for this function - the latter have, in law, powers of attorney on behalf of veterans seeking benefits.

There are 58 Veterans Administration offices, one in each state and a few abroad. The Administration is proud of the fact that these offices are "one-stop shopping centres" which counsel on, and receive applications for all the sub-programs of the Administration. When a serviceman leaves the Service, his basic information is automatically entered in the Administration data bank.

Action flow on applications for all benefits is as follows:

a. application is made to one of the 58 Administration offices;
b. the application is assessed by the office Adjudication Division;
c. any first appeal is returned to the same Adjudication Division where, normally, new adjudicators then deal with the case; and
d. second appeals go to the Appeal Board (normally consisting of 1 physician and 2 attorneys). Veterans may appear in person but, if so, must pay their own way. The Board travels to each State at intervals of 12-18 months.

The Administration has resisted all pressures to use private sector facilities on the basis that the quality of service would be much reduced without any significant savings.

A proposal has been made to centralize Rating (adjudication) Boards in three regional offices. The Administration sees this as expensive and as leading to a reduction in the quality of service . The likelihood of such a decision being made is seen as remote.

Although there are several differences between Canadian and U.S. benefits for veterans, on balance it is considered that Canada is at least as generous as the U.S. toward her veterans.

The major advantage of the U.S. system which has an application for Canada is the fully integrated decentralized structure which provides a better service to veterans.

RECORD OF CONSULTATION

There were two types of consultation carried out during the study. The first was with organizations representing veterans, and the second was with other organizations which had similar clientele or had done research in an area of particular interest.

CONSULTATION WITH VETERANS' ORGANIZATIONS

At the beginning of the study, the team leader met with Mr. Clifford Chadderton, Chairman of the National Council of Veteran Associations and Mr. Colin Graham, Dominion Secretary of the Royal Canadian Legion. Both officials stated their position as being in favour of any change which would improve the service to veterans, particularly for disability pensions.

CONSULTATIONS WITH OTHER ORGANIZATIONS

Consultations on health care for senior citizens took place with:

Mrs. Evelyn Shapiro, Chairman, Manitoba Health Services and Professor, Faculty of Medicine, University of Manitoba

Dr. Betty Havens, Provincial Gerontologist, Province of Manitoba

Mr. Eckhard Goerz, Program Specialist, Health Department, Province of Manitoba

The area of discussion was forecasting the need of an aging population for "home care" and "institutional care". These three people supped information based on special studies carried out by, and the experiences of, the Province of Manitoba. This information was used in the forecasts of workload for the Veterans Affairs portfolio.

Consultations also took place with Dr. Hannah Sellers of the Disability Division (Canada Pension Plan) of the Income Security Programs of the Department of National Health and Welfare. This division handles disability pensions under the Canada Pension Plan. The administration requirements are very similar to those of the Canadian Pension Commission. While this division had some backlog problems which it was currently addressing, they were

operating in a much simpler and faster mode than the
Canadian Pension Commission. The recommendations of the
study team were influenced by the better administrative
arrangements of the Canada Pension Plan.

The headquarters of the U.S. Veterans Administration in
Washington was visited and the results of the visit given in
the report. The "single" administration of the U.S.
Veterans Administration was the most significant finding.